DrawPlus X3 User Guide

How to Contact Us

Our main office
(UK, Europe):

The Software Centre
PO Box 2000, Nottingham,
NG11 7GW, UK

Main:	(0115) 914 2000
Registration (UK only):	(0800) 376 1989
Sales (UK only):	(0800) 376 7070
Customer Service/ Technical Support:	http://www.serif.com/support
General Fax:	(0115) 914 2020

North American office
(USA, Canada):

The Software Center
13 Columbia Drive, Suite 5, Amherst
NH 03031, USA

Main:	(603) 889-8650
Registration:	(800) 794-6876
Sales:	(800) 55-SERIF or 557-3743
Customer Service/ Technical Support:	http://www.serif.com/support
General Fax:	(603) 889-1127

Online

Visit us on the web at: http://www.serif.com/

International

Please contact your local distributor/dealer. For further details, please contact us at one of our phone numbers above.

Contents

Contents

Contents

Welcome

Welcome

1

Welcome to **DRAW**PLUS X3
Graphics Studio

Welcome to **DrawPlus X3**—the design and illustration solution from Serif, fully certified for Windows Vista, and packed with all the features expected of award-winning design software. From decorative page elements and logos to full-page illustrations, scale drawings, multi-page publications, and Stopframe or Keyframe animations— DrawPlus X3 does it all. With the power of scalable vector graphics at your command, you'll see the creative possibilities open up right before your eyes! Whether you're a beginner or an expert, you'll find easy-to-use tools you can use right away. With this version, DrawPlus has broken the price-performance barrier once again!

If you've upgraded from a previous version, this new edition of DrawPlus includes a host of **exciting new features** (see p. 12) which complement the **key features** listed overleaf.

Don't forget to register your new copy, using the **Registration Wizard** on the **Help** menu. That way, we can keep you informed of new developments and future upgrades!

Key features

Document

- **Multipage Document Support**
  From startup to printout, the versatile DrawPlus engine sustains your creativity. Choose from a wide range of preset document types, including **booklets** and folded **documents**. Work on pages right side up... automatic imposition assures correct order and orientation of your output. Use DrawPlus's always-at-hand collection of popular design templates to create designs quickly.

- **Import PDF**
  Unlock the contents of third-party PDF drawings using DrawPlus's impressive "open PDF" feature—objects can be brought into a new drawing with a single-click for immediate editing.

- **Layers**
  Each page can have multiple layers so you can assign elements to different layers for modular design. Each layer entry hosts a hierarchical tree view of associated thumbnailed objects.

- **Rotate Canvas**
  Let your canvas rotate through any angle, just like an artist would do in real-life. Great for artists with tablets, for drawing freeform curves at any orientation, and for getting a different perspective of your drawing!

- **Pseudo 3D Projections**
  Project objects isometrically onto Top, Front, or Right planes via a Standard toolbar. For more advanced projections, take advantage of editable Dimetric, Trimetric, Oblique projections, or even create your own **Custom** projection.

- **View Quality**
  Draw in one of several drawing modes to view objects at optimum quality (**Normal** mode), unsmoothed (**Draft**) or as single-pixel outlines (**Wireframe**).

- **Professional-Standard Drawing Features**
  Features like converting text to curves, defining custom envelopes, fully customizable drop shadows, layers, and scalable vector graphics give complete creative power. Combine two shapes into one... Subtract for cropping and masking... Intersect to carve out unique shapes and regions.

Design

- **Cropping**
  Any object can serve as a "cookie cutter" for trimming one or more other objects into a single shape... and the effect is reversible so you won't lose your originals. Great for creating "reflections" of complex scenes!

- **Vector editing tools**
  Tools such as Knife Tool cuts through objects, leaving them in multiple parts, still as vectors. The Erase Tool removes areas under a brush line of variable nib width to redefine object boundaries! The opposite of the **Erase Tool**, the **Freeform Paint Tool** "adds to" current vector objects (shapes, text, bitmaps).

- **Comprehensive Design Gallery**
  The Gallery tab provides an impressive selection of instantly available Arts & Crafts, Cartoons, ShapeArt, Connecting Symbols (family trees, electronics, computers), and Layout Symbols (garden and interior design), and many more. Use the Gallery to additionally store and organize your own favourite designs for future use!

- **Picture Import and Adjustments**
  Import pictures from hard disk, CD/DVD, PhotoCD, digital camera or scanner. Use image adjustments for quick fixes (or special effects) including Red Eye Tool, Auto Levels, Auto Contrast, Brightness/Contrast, and many more. Apply adjustments singularly or in combination.

- **Object Default control**
  Set your intended object's default line colour/style, fill, and transparency before even drawing your object! As a more powerful default control, Synchronize Defaults lets you adopt a currently selected object's attributes for future objects; For example, select a red brush stroke, to subsequently paint in red, then a green brush stroke to paint in green; all or selected attributes can be affected. Global and object-specific defaults can be reset independently.

- **Resource Management**
  Swap out your already placed bitmaps or text fragments in Drawing mode or any Animation mode from the new **Media tab**; a Keyframe animation's movie or audio clip can also be replaced.

Colour and Transparency

- **Design Power with Colour Gradient Fills**
  The Gradient Fill Editor allows you to adjust gradient contour and tint any portion of the colour spread, locate key colours precisely... and select from RGB, HSL, CMYK, PANTONE® or Registration colours via a Colour Selector.

- **Advanced Fill Support**
  Simply apply solid colours from the Studio's Colour tab or Swatches tab onto a fill path to add or replace colours for more subtle gradients. Choose colours from different colour mixing modes in the Colour tab—**HSL Wheel, HSL Square, RGB Sliders, CMYK Sliders** or Tinting all offer different ways to mix colour. Load RGB, CMYK and coordinated "themed" palettes from within the Swatches tab. Apply high-end linear, radial, conical, ellipse, three colour, four colour, square, and plasma fills to any text or shape for exciting, professional results. Use bitmap fills for textures and backgrounds. Add, view, edit, or delete colours used in your current drawing from within a saveable **Document Palette**. Even import your own bitmaps and use them as fills on DrawPlus objects! Plus Mesh Fills for impressively varied gradients using a path-node network. Define new colour sets based on a base colour—this linkage can transform the drawing's colour scheme instantly, by simply modifying that base colour!

- **Transparency Effects**
  Transparency can make the difference between flat, ordinary visuals and sparkling realism! And DrawPlus provides it all—a full range of transparencies for shading, shadows, reflections, depth effects, and more.

Lines, brushes, and shapes

- **Versatile Line Drawing**
  Sketch using calligraphic lines with an adjustable pen angle. Add rounded corners when and where you need them... and choose different end caps and joins. Create decorative **chain lines** for marching footprints, themed borders, and much more.

- **Dimension Lines and Scale Setting**
  Click a couple of times to take linear or angular measurements of any object on the page—DrawPlus displays the dimension using your choice of ruler units, at your specified scale (say, one inch to two feet). Dimensions update when objects are moved or resized! Design room layouts, make maps, draw scale models, and more.

- **Connectors**
  For drawing dynamic flow diagrams, schematics, family trees, and organization charts, connector objects let you link your boxes and symbols and then rearrange at will. Connection points stay put on each object... keeping connections intact. **Auto Connectors** intelligently display bridges at line crossings, and even route themselves around obstructive objects.

- **Natural Curve Editing**
  Simply click and drag to break and redraw a curve at any node. Apply smoothing selectively to freeform curves to eliminate that "shaky hand" appearance.

- **Intelligent Curve Tracing**
  Simply "connect the dots" to trace around curved objects and pictures... the **Pen Tool** features Smart segments that use automatic curve-fitting to connect each node!

- **Brushes**

  Unleash the painter within you, with DrawPlus's powerful **Paintbrush Tool** and the supporting Brush tab's galleries! Pick from natural media brush types such as acrylic, charcoal, dry paint, pastel, pen, and watercolour, or create your own. Using a pressure-sensitive pen tablet? **Pressure sensitivity** is supported (via a Pressure tab) with preset or custom pressure profiles and control over the maximum and minimum pressure applied.

- **QuickShapes**

  QuickShapes work like intelligent clipart… or the most powerful set of drawing tools you've ever envisaged. Even extremely complex shapes like spirals, stars, and webs are simple to draw and customize using QuickShapes. Type text directly into any shape!

Text

- **Working with Text**

  Apply and edit artistic, frame, or shape text right on the page… apply basic formatting from the always-at-hand Text context toolbar. Control advanced properties like text flow (wrap), kerning, leading, paragraph indents, above/below spacing. Need foreign language support? Simply paste text in Unicode format as either formatted RTF or unformatted plain text. Font substitutions during the opening of DrawPlus or PDF files offers an interactive means of managing missing fonts. Use **Spell Checker** to proof your output—check any text against an editable user dictionary.

Effects

- **Perform Powerful Blends**

  The **Blend Tool** allows adjustment of blend steps, transform, and attribute profiles (rate of change). Objects can be multiply-blended (to/from other blends) to create truly stunning illustrations.

- **Instant 3D with on-screen transforms**

  Transform 3D objects with in-situ 3D rotational control and editing. Apply awesome multi-coloured **lighting effects** (with directional control), along with custom **bevel** and **lathe** effect profiles to create your very own unique contours. **Hardware-accelerated rendering** boosts redraw performance (hardware dependent).

- **Perspective Effects**
  Get a new slant on things... With a context toolbar flyout full of presets plus a built-in tool for freeform adjustments, the **Perspective Tool** lets you tilt and skew text (or any other object) for truly "spatial" results!

- **Roughen Tool**
  For jagged, jaunty edges on text, lines, or QuickShapes, just drag the tool up or down for subtle or bold results.

- **Border Wizard**
  Vastly flexible **Border Wizard** instantly adds borders to the page or to individual objects. Choose a border from the extensive library, or be creative and let Border Wizard guide you through building a unique design.

- **Filter Effects**
  Drop shadows starting to wear a bit thin? Enliven your text with fully adjustable **Inner Shadow**, **Glow**, **Bevel**, and **Emboss** filters... easy to apply and sure to impress. Apply soft edges with the Feathering filter effect—great for blends, montages, vignetted photo borders, and much more.

- **Astounding 3D Lighting and Surface Effects**
  Advanced algorithms bring flat shapes to life! Choose one or more effects, then vary surface and source light properties. Adjust parameters for incredible surface contours, textures, fills. The Studio's **Effects Tab** offers preset 3D effects you can apply and customize as you wish.

Web and Animation

- **Web Image Slices, Image Maps, Rollover States**
  Beat the pros at their own game by using these techniques to add links to your Web graphics! With a few clicks, divide images into segments—each with its own hyperlink and popup text—or add hotspots to specific regions. Even let DrawPlus create interactive rollover Web graphics that highlight or change state when users mouse over or click!

- **Stopframe Animation**
  Tap the power of QuickShapes to turn out Web **stopframe** animations in no time—using advanced features like onion skinning, backgrounds, overlays, and frame management.

- **Keyframe Animation**
  Produce smooth, professional and quick-to-design animations as **Adobe® Flash®** files, all from within the Storyboard tab. The **Easing tab** defines editable envelope profiles for defining the rate of change of an object's transformation and attributes. The **Actions tab** can assign "events" (mouse click, hover over, and many more) and an associated action (e.g., jump to a named URL or animation marker); develop directly in **ActionScript** for the more adventurous! Use the **Keyframe Camera** to pan, zoom, or rotate around your animation's keyframes. Add **sound** and **movies** to any Keyframe animation. Export to Flash, Flash Lite/i-Mode, screensaver or a choice of video formats.

Export and Print

- **Image Export Optimizer**
  The **Export Optimizer** lets you see how your image will look (and how much space it will take up) before you save it! Its multi-window display provides side-by-side WYSIWYG previews of image quality at various output settings, so you can make the best choice every time. Use **Dynamic Preview** to work in an **edit-and-preview** mode at a given DPI, file format, and number of colours.

- **PDF Export**
  Step up to the worldwide standard for cross-platform, WYSIWYG electronic information delivery. Your **PDF output** will look just like your DrawPlus document... in one compact package with embeddable fonts, easily printable or viewable in a Web browser.

- **Professional Print Output**

  PDF publishing to the **PDF/X-1** or **PDF/X-1a** file format is a great choice for professional output from DrawPlus. Deliver with confidence to your print partner, safe in the knowledge that your single composite print-ready PDF drawing includes all fonts and colour information for spot or process colour separation. Select file information, crop marks, registration targets, and densitometer/colour calibration bars for inclusion in your PDF. Spot or process colour (CMYK) separations for full colour printing are possible. You have full control over prepress settings for output.

New features in DrawPlus X3

Images

- **AutoTrace** (p. 179)
  Convert bitmaps to vector art with **AutoTrace** studio. Adopt **preset profiles** for optimum tracing of **bitmapped logos**, as well as **colour** and **black and white photos**. Create your own **custom profiles** for tracing files with similar characteristics. Use **adjustment tools** for fine-tuning traced output (add/remove colours, merge areas, smooth curves, or erase nodes).

- **Quick-and-easy image cutouts** (p. 173)
  Image Cutout Studio makes light work of cutting out your placed images, directly within DrawPlus. Use brushes to discard uniform backgrounds (sky, walls, etc.) or keep subjects of interest (people, objects, etc.). Two output types—**Alpha-edged Bitmap** or **Vector-cropped Bitmap**—offer transparency blending or feathering techniques at the cutout edge to seamlessly merge your image with your page.

Ease of Use

- **Opacity control in Colour tab** (p. 162)
  For improved productivity, any colour chosen in DrawPlus can now have an associated **Opacity** applied at the same time. Great for setting colour/opacity combinations on objects or nodes on fill paths!

- **Improved toolbars**
  The **Standard** toolbar now sports large icons for better visual cues, and hosts the now always-at-hand **3D Planes** and **Overlays** options for perspective drawing and design aids.

- **Lasso selection** (p. 55)
  Difficulty selecting complex objects? For better control, use the **Alt** key with your Pointer Tool and draw a lasso around objects. Even lasso nodes while editing curves.

Design

- **Spray brush strokes** (p. 81)
  Have some painting fun with spray brushes from categories such as **Airbrushes**, **Grunge**, and **Special Effects**; change brush colours to suit your design or adjust brush nozzle control.

- **Brush and edge effects on object outlines** (p. 147)
  Bored of solid line fills? Try **stroking a brush outline** around artistic text, image, and shapes. Alternatively, use **textured edge brushes** for ripped, painted, smudged, glowing or burnt edges.

- **Design aids** (p. 42)
  Use Overlays such as **Rule of Thirds** grid (for improved page composition) and **Divine Proportions** (for aesthetic proportioning). For more focused design, use **Solo mode** to work on an object in isolation.

- **New stunning 2D and 3D filter effects** (p. 193 and p. 196)
  Blur any object or create a coloured solid or gradient **outline** around object edges (use the new Contour fill which applies gradient fill from the inner to outer outline width). **3D effects** are boosted with **Reflection Maps** which offer a realistic glass-like transparency control of non-reflective/reflective surfaces. Multiple separately coloured lights are added for dramatic **lighting effects**. All filter effects can now be applied in preview mode or to the object on the page.

- **Powerful object cropping** (p. 110)
  The **Crop Tool** makes cropping your design or imported image more instinctive and intuitive. An on-document control bar lets you transform the crop window, with respect to position, rotation, and shape. Crop to preset Crop Shapes. For better composition while cropping, use a cropping Rule Thirds grid.

Importing and Exporting

- **Open picture as document** (p. 24)
  Pictures can now be opened in DrawPlus as a new document automatically sized to the picture dimensions. Add design objects (captions, line, or shapes) and then export.

- **Export selected regions** (p. 252)

  Easily draw and size an overlay region around an area of your design, then export it via Export Optimizer!

- **HD Photo and PostScript files** (p. 171)

  Import and export as Microsoft's new HD Photo file format! Import Encapsulated PostScript files (.eps) as well.

- **Open Adobe Illustrator files** (p. 25)

  Open and edit Adobe Illustrator files (9.0 and above) directly into DrawPlus.

- **A new metafile format** (p. 171)

  Import and export Serif Metafiles (.SMF), a proprietary image format with improvements to the Windows Metafile format (WMF). Better line, fill, and text definitions make them ideal for sharing graphics between Serif applications.

Sharing

- **Share your designs online!** (p. 255)

  Upload your DrawPlus design to the community website, **www.drawplus.com**. View designs using powerful zoom technology, give a star rating, comment on, or search for any design by tag. Create public or private groups for like-minded designers—great for making new friends! Take part in design forum discussions.

..and some other enhancements you've requested

- The new **Arrange tab** consolidates all your tools for object ordering, flipping, cropping, combining, and joining. Export Optimizer now shows all export settings. Create and scale objects from their centres. The Knife Tool has been "sharpened up" with different **cutting types** (square, zig-zag, wave, and more) and preset **cookie cutter shapes** (ellipses, rectangles, stars, and more). Easily apply **Material Thickness** and a **Feather Edge** directly via the Effects tab. Brushes now include photo-based stitches, laces, zippers, and spray effects. Now manipulate **transparent bitmap outlines** instead of the bitmap's bounding box.

Installation

System Requirements

Minimum:

- Windows-based PC with DVD/CD drive and mouse

- Microsoft Windows® XP or Vista operating system

- 512MB RAM

- 375MB (recommended full install) free hard disk space

- 1024x768 monitor resolution

Additional disk resources and memory are required when editing large or complex documents.

> To enjoy the full benefit of brushes and their textures, you must be using a computer whose processor supports SSE (most modern computers do). On brush selection, an on-screen message will indicate if your computer is non-SSE.

Recommended:

As above but:

- Multi-processor PC technology

Optional:

- Windows-compatible printer

- TWAIN-compatible scanner and/or digital camera

- Pressure-sensitive pen tablet (Serif GraphicsPad or equivalent)

- 3D accelerated graphics card with DirectX 9 (or above) or OpenGL support

- Internet account and connection required for accessing online resources

First-time install

To install DrawPlus X3 simply insert the DrawPlus X3 Program CD into your DVD/CD drive. The AutoRun feature automatically starts the Setup process. (If it doesn't, follow the manual install procedure described below.) Just answer the on-screen questions to install the program.

Manual install/re-install

To re-install the software or to change the installation at a later date, select **Settings/Control Panel** from the Windows Start menu and then click on the **Add/Remove Programs** icon. Make sure the DrawPlus X3 Program CD is inserted into your CD/DVD drive, click the **Install...** button and then simply follow the on-screen instructions.

Getting Started

2

Startup Wizard

Once DrawPlus has been installed, you're ready to start. Setup adds a **Serif DrawPlus X3** item to the **All Programs** submenu of the Windows **Start** menu.

- Use the Windows **Start** button to start DrawPlus (or if DrawPlus is already running, choose **New>New from Startup Wizard...** from the File menu) to display the Startup Wizard.

The Startup Wizard offers different routes into the program for you to explore:

The above options are described as follows:

Create		Allows you to....
	Start New Drawing	create a drawing from scratch
	Keyframe Animation	create a Keyframe animation in Keyframe animation mode
	Stopframe Animation	create a Stopframe animation in Stopframe animation mode

Open		
	Open Saved Work	open and edit your saved DrawPlus drawings
	Design Template	create an instant drawing or animation from a design
	Import PDF	create a design from an existing PDF file.
View		
	Sample Designs	load some example drawing files to boost your imagination!
	Browse Tutorials	access the DrawPlus tutorials
	Online Videos	View a selection of online product videos

Use the **Choose Workspace** drop-down menu to choose your workspace appearance (i.e., Studio tab positions, tab sizes, and show/hide tab status). You can adopt the default workspace profile <**Default Profile**>, the last used profile <**Current Profile**>, a range of profile presets, or a workspace profile you've previously saved.

The Startup Wizard is displayed by default when you launch DrawPlus. If you don't want to use the Startup Wizard again, check the "Don't show this wizard again" box. You can switch it on again via **Startup Wizard** in **Tools>Options...** (use Ease of Use menu option).

You can also access the Startup Wizard at any time from **New>New from Startup Wizard...** on the **File** menu.

Starting with a design template

It's so much easier creating drawings with a little bit of help—DrawPlus can utilize a whole range of **design templates** which will speed you through the creation of all types of drawings and animations! Templates can be thought of as "object factories." They let you pick a design and leave you with one or more new objects on the page.

If the design is exactly what you want then all that is left is for you to print it or export it. If you want to personalize the design or add to it then you need to know how to work with objects (see p. 105)!

An impressive range of templates categories are at you disposal. Choose from categories such as Arts & Crafts, Logos, Posters, Web Banners, and Greeting Cards.

To create a drawing from a Design Template:

1. Launch DrawPlus, or choose **New>New from Startup Wizard...** from the **File** menu. You'll see the Startup Wizard.

2. Select **Open>Design Template**.

3.   From the dialog, select a drawing category on the left, and examine the designs on the right. Click the thumbnail that's closest to the one you want, then click **Open**.

The design is loaded and forms the basis of your new **unsaved** drawing or animation. When you make any changes, you'll be prompted to save the drawing or animation to a file name.

> ★   You can save any drawing or animation as a template (see Saving templates; p. 27) at any time.

Starting with a new drawing

The first time you launch DrawPlus, you'll see the **Startup Wizard**, with a menu of choices. The **Start New Drawing** option offers an easy way to create your new drawing and takes care of the initial setup for the particular type of document you'll be producing.

Choose from a wide range of preset document types, including **booklets** and folded **documents**. Work on pages right side up... automatic imposition assures correct order and orientation of your output.

To start a new drawing from scratch using the Startup Wizard:

1.   Start DrawPlus (or choose **File>New>New from Startup Wizard...** if it's already running).

2.   Select **Start New Drawing** from the Startup Wizard.

3.   Select a document category from the Documents pane (and a sub-category if applicable). Categories contain preset document types or if you select **Regular**, you can choose from standard document sizes presented in Portrait or Landscape sub-categories. For custom sized pages, choose the **Custom Page Setup** button at the bottom of the dialog.

4.   Select a document type thumbnail from the right-hand pane and click **Open**. The new document opens.

> ★   The **My Templates** category lets you base your new drawing on a previously saved template.

To start a new drawing during your DrawPlus session:

- Click **New Drawing** on the **Standard** toolbar (if Startup Wizard is disabled).

  - or -

  Choose **New>New Drawing** from the **File** menu.

You'll get a new drawing in a new untitled window each time you choose this method—the default page size is adopted.

> ★ You can always adjust the page size and document format later via **File>Page Setup...**.

To turn on/off the Startup Wizard:

1. Choose **Options...** from the **Tools** menu.

2. Click **Ease of Use** and check/uncheck **Startup Wizard**.

> ★ To start with a new animation, see Getting started with animation on p. 207.
>
> 💡 Use Import PDF from the Startup Wizard to unlock the contents of third-party PDF drawings.

Opening a saved document

You can open an existing DrawPlus drawing from the Startup Wizard, **Standard** toolbar or the **File** menu. Once open, drawings can be made currently active from a drawing tab or via the Window menu.

To open an existing document from the Startup Wizard:

1. Select **Open Saved Work** option. In the Documents pane of the **Open Saved Work** dialog, you'll see either your computer's folder structure for navigation to your DrawPlus drawings (Folders tab) or a list of most recently used drawings (History tab). Preview thumbnails are shown in the adjacent pane.

2. Select a thumbnail from the pane, then click **Open**.

To open an existing document via toolbar or menu:

1.   Click 📁 **Open** on the **Standard** toolbar, or select **File>Open...**.

2.   In the Open dialog, navigate to, then select the file name and click the **Open** button.

Displaying drawings

<u>1</u> Drawing1
✓ <u>2</u> Peppers *
<u>3</u> Blend2 *

If you open multiple drawings at the same time, you can easily jump between drawings by selecting a drawing name from the Window menu. Unsaved drawings are indicated by an asterisk; the currently active document is shown with a tick.

📄 Blend2 *   📄 Drawing1   📄 Peppers *

Alternatively, you can simply click on an open drawing's tab at the top of the workspace to make it active (e.g., the unsaved drawing "Peppers"). Drawings that are not active are greyed out.

Opening other file types

Opening images as a new document

DrawPlus allows a comprehensive range of image file formats to be opened, each as a separate DrawPlus document. From the document, you can add your own text captions, lines, shapes, or simply make image adjustments. You can save your design changes as a new project or just export the image (with or without adjustment), while preserving its original properties.

To open an image:

1. Click **Open** on the **Standard** toolbar.

2. Change the file type drop-down menu to display **All Image Files**, locate and select the file, and click **Open**. The image occupies your workspace such that page dimensions are adjusted to match the image dimensions (a **Custom** page size is adopted; in pixels).

3. (Optional) You can modify the image—modify the document as for any other document or double-click the image to load the Image Adjustment dialog (then apply one or more adjustments).

4. Click **Save** to save the document as a DrawPlus .dpp project, or **File>Export>Export as Image...** to export it to the same or a different file format (the original image's name, dpi, colour depth, and transparency settings are maintained for export).

Opening PDF and Adobe Illustrator files

It is possible to open PDF and Adobe Illustrator files—once opened you can save the either file format as a DrawPlus Drawing (.DPP). The character formatting, layout and images in the original document are preserved to allow for editing of the imported content.

To open a PDF or Adobe Illustrator file:

1. Click **Open** on the **Standard** toolbar.

> ★ For PDF files, you can also select **Import PDF** from the Startup Wizard.

2. From the dialog, navigate to, then select the file, and click **Open**. The document is loaded and the drawing will repaginate to the number of pages of the original document if multi-page (PDF only).

Opening AutoCAD files

DrawPlus opens AutoCAD® .dwg and .dxf files quickly and easily. Using the same process as that for PDF files, this creates an opportunity to not only view engineering layouts and designs (up to AutoCAD 2006) in DrawPlus, but to edit the drawn objects and to save the drawing as a DrawPlus Drawing (.DPP).

On file open, a **DXF/DWG Options** dialog provides options to scale the imported file objects, position the artwork on the page and merge objects onto one layer.

To open an AutoCAD file:

1. Click ![open folder icon] **Open** on the **Standard** toolbar.

2. Change the file type drop-down menu to display **AutoCAD files** (*.dwg,*.dxf), locate and select the file, and click **Open**.

3. In the dialog, specify scaling and positioning options. Uncheck **Merge Layers** to retain the layer structure of the original AutoCAD file—layers will automatically be shown in the Layers tab.

4. Click **OK**. The AutoCAD drawing is imported.

Saving your work

DrawPlus saves its documents as .dpp (Drawing), .dpx (Template) or .dpa (Animation) files (for Stopframe and Keyframe animation modes).

To save your work:

- Click ![save icon] **Save** on the **Standard** toolbar.

  - or -

  To save the document under its current name, choose **Save...** from the **File** menu.

  - or -

  To save under a different name, choose **Save As...** from the **File** menu.

Saving templates

If you've decided that a particular design might be useful in future you can save the layout as a **template**. You can save any DrawPlus drawing as a template (*.dpx) file. When opening a saved template file, DrawPlus automatically opens an untitled copy, leaving the original template intact.

To save a drawing as a template:

1. Choose **Save As...** from the **File** menu. Under "Save as type:" select the **DrawPlus Template (*.dpx)** option. By default, the template will be saved to a "My Templates" folder so that your templates will be accessible for future use (see Starting with a new drawing on p. 22).

2. Enter a file name, leaving the file extension intact, and click **Save**.

To edit a template file directly:

1. Choose **Open...** from the **File** menu and select **DrawPlus Templates (*.dpx)** in the "Files of type:" box.

2. Navigate to the folder containing your saved template file and select it.

3. To open the original template, uncheck the **Open as untitled** option.

4. Click the **Open** button. You can then make edits to your template.

Closing DrawPlus

To close the current document:

- Choose **Close** from the **File** menu or click the window's ⊠ **Close** button.

  - or -

  If you have a middle mouse button (wheel), click it when you hover over the document tab at the top of your workspace.

If the document is still unsaved or there are unsaved changes, you'll be prompted to save changes.

To close DrawPlus:

- Choose **Exit** from the **File** menu.

For each open window, you'll be prompted to save any changes made since the last save.

Working with Pages

3

Setting up a document

A document's page size and orientation settings make a fundamental difference
to its layout, and are defined when the new document is first created (see
Starting with a new drawing on p. 22). If the Startup Wizard is turned off, or you
cancel the setup dialog, a new document defaults to A4 (Europe) or Letter size
(US) in Drawing Mode. You can adjust the document layout at any time—but as
a general rule, it's best to make page setup one of your first creative tasks.

For scale drawings, you can set the ruler units independently of the page
measurement units. See Setting measurement units and drawing scale.

To adjust the basic layout of the document (Drawing mode):

1. Choose [★ Page Setup] from the context toolbar (shown with
   Pointer or Rotate Tool selected).

2. Select a document category: Regular, Large (for example, banners or
   posters), Small (for example, business cards), Booklet, or Special
   Folded (greetings cards).

   • Where applicable, click in the document list to preview available
     formats for the selected category. Watch the preview window for
     an example of each type.

   • If you select Large or Small, you can define a custom document
     format by clicking Create Custom... and entering the desired
     settings.

   • If you select Regular or Booklet, you can check Facing Pages to
     set up the document using paired, side-by-side pages. This is
     appropriate if you're creating a document where you need to see
     both the left-hand (verso) and right-hand (recto) pages, or one
     that employs double-page spreads where a headline or other
     element needs to run from the left-hand page to the right-hand
     page.

3. Select a **Document Size**, set the orientation (Portrait or Landscape)
   and enter a Width and Height (if a custom setup).
   You can change this later via the Pages context toolbar.

4.   Adjust the document **Margins** to your specifications. You can set the left, right, top, and bottom margins individually, or click the **From Printer** button to derive the page margin settings from the current printer settings. The dialog also provides options for **Balanced** margins (left matching right, top matching bottom) or for two **Mirrored** margins on facing pages where the "left" margin setting becomes the "inside," and the "right" margin becomes the "outside."

Using the page and pasteboard

Most of the DrawPlus display is taken up by a **page** or "artwork" area and a surrounding **pasteboard** area. This arrangement is an electronic equivalent of the system used by traditional graphic designers. They kept design tools and bits of text and graphics on a large pasteboard, and then carefully pasted final arrangements of text and graphics onto a page-sized "artwork" sheet pinned down in the middle of the board.

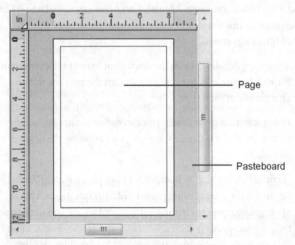

Page

Pasteboard

The **page area** is where you put the text and graphic elements that you want to be part of the final output. The **pasteboard area** is where you generally keep any elements that are being prepared or waiting to be positioned on the page area.

Setting measurement units and drawing scale

For precision drawing, you need techniques that allow you to position and draw accurately without effort, which will also be of use at any scaled size. Such techniques make use of rulers and guides for actual-size or scaled drawings.

Rulers

The DrawPlus rulers mimic the paste-up artist's T-square, and acts as a measuring tool and guide creator. The rulers that surround the page allow you to measure the exact position of an object.

Ruler units used by DrawPlus determine the units displayed on the rulers and the reported units shown when positioning and scaling objects (either around the object or on the **Hintline**). You can change the ruler units without altering the document's dimensions. Unit settings are saved with your DrawPlus document; as a result loading different documents, templates, etc. may change your working measurement units.

To change the page unit:

- Choose **Options...** from the **Tools** menu and click **Layout**, then make a selection in the **Ruler Units** box.

> Ruler Units are equivalent to Page Units unless you're working on a scale drawing. For example, at 100% zoom, one ruler centimetre equals one centimetre on the printed page

Moving rulers

By default, the horizontal ruler lies along the top of the DrawPlus window and the vertical ruler along the left edge. The default **ruler intersection** is the top-left corner of the pasteboard area. The default **zero point** (marked as 0 on each ruler) is the top-left corner of the page area.

To move either ruler to a different position, click and drag on the ruler intersection button (showing the type of measurement unit).

The small tab ⊿ that is shown on the intersection button can be used to set a new ruler origin—simply drag the tab onto the page and release to set the position of your new origin (cross-hair guides and the **Hintline** toolbar help this positioning). Double-click on the intersection to reset the origin back to its default position. All guide positions are recalculated as the origin changes position.

Double-click on the ruler intersection to make the rulers' zero point jump to the top left-hand corner of the selected object.

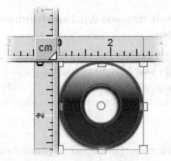

This comes in handy for measuring page objects. If the rulers have already been moved or the object is deselected, double-clicking on the intersection will send the rulers back to the default position.

Rulers as a measuring tool

The most obvious role for rulers is as a measuring tool. As you move the mouse pointer, a small line marker along each ruler displays the current horizontal and vertical cursor position. When you select an object the rulers not only show its position, but also its extent by a lighter coloured area (also showing the object's dimensions).

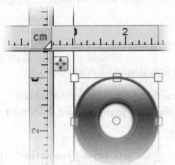

Creating guides

If you want to position objects repeatedly on the same horizontal or vertical boundary then **guides** can be used. DrawPlus lets you set up horizontal and vertical **guides**—non-printing, red lines you can use to align one object with another. Guides are "sticky" as long as you have **Snap to Guides** turned on (via **Tools>Options>Snapping**), i.e. a moved object will behave as if it is attracted to a guide as you move it close to the line. Guides also attract the object when you are changing its size.

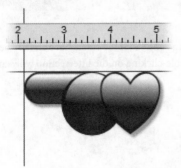

To create a guide:

- For a horizontal or vertical guide, click on the horizontal or vertical ruler, respectively, and drag onto the page while fine-tuning the guide into its position.

> ★ Hold down the **Alt** key before guide creation to produce a horizontal guide from a vertical ruler and vice versa.

To move, delete and lock guides:

- To **move** a guide, click and drag it into position with the Pointer Tool.

- To **remove** a guide, drag and drop it onto the respective ruler.

- To **lock** the guides and prevent them from being moved, choose **Options...** from the **Tools** menu, click **Snapping**, and check the **Lock Guides** box (or right-click on a ruler).

- To **show** or **hide** guides, check or uncheck **Layout Tools>Guides** from the **View** menu.

Drawing scale

You can create **scale drawings** (such as a house plan or model diagram) by setting a ratio other than 1:1 between page units and ruler units. For example, you might wish to set one page inch equivalent to ten (ruler) feet.

> ★ Right-click anywhere on your rulers to quickly swap to a different unit of measurement—the rulers and Transform tab are updated instantly.

To change the drawing scale:

1. Choose 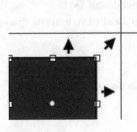 from the context toolbar (shown with Pointer or Rotate Tool selected).

2. Check the **Scale Drawing** box.

> ☑ Scale Drawing
>
> Page Distance: Ruler Distance:
>
> 1.00 ⬍ Inches ▼ = 10.00 ⬍ Feet ▼
>
> Printed page size: 8.268in x 11.693in
> Scaled page size: 82.677ft x 116.929ft

3. Use the input boxes to set the drawing scale as a proportion between the Page Distance (in **page units** that define the document's actual printing dimensions) and the Ruler Distance (in on-screen **ruler units** that represent the "real world" objects you're depicting). Units and object dimensions update and scale accordingly.

Using snapping

With **Snapping** enabled, objects you create, move, or resize will jump to align with nearby, visible guides or a defined grid, respectively. For snapping to guides, think of an object as being broken into four quadrants such that you drag from the object's upper right quadrant (below) towards the guides to produce the "snapping" effect.

To turn snapping on and off:

1. Choose ⊞ Snapping from the context toolbar (shown with Pointer or Rotate Tool selected).

2. In the Snapping pane, check or uncheck the **Snapping** box.

Snapping   Change snapping preferences

  Grid Spacing

Horizontal   8.00 ⬍ lines per in   Subdivisions: 5 ⬍

Vertical   8.00 ⬍ lines per in   Subdivisions: 5 ⬍

☑ Snapping   Options

                   ☑ Display Guides   Guide Colour ▬ ▾

   ☑ Snap to Guides   ☐ Display Grid   Grid Colour ▬ ▾

   ☐ Snap to Grid   ☐ Lock Guides   Grid Style   Lines ▾

                                             ☑ Draw Grid Behind

💡   Alternatively, switch Snapping on or off via the Arrange menu.

To snap to guides and/or grid:

- With the Snapping option checked, check the **Snap to Guides** and/or **Snap to Grid** option in **Tools>Options>Snapping**.

If you find snapping bothersome, it may be that you have the grid spacing set too coarsely to allow you the freedom you need in your design. Go to **Tools>Options>Snapping** to set a finer horizontal and/or vertical grid spacing (you can also change grid colour and style).

To show or hide the snapping grid:

- Choose **Layout Tools** from the **View** menu and check or uncheck **Snapping Grid** on the submenu.

  - or -

  Choose **Options...** from the **Tools** menu and click **Snapping**, then check or uncheck the **Display Grid** box.

Viewing pages

The HintLine toolbar at the bottom of the screen displays the current page number and provides a number of controls to let you navigate around your pages. As an alternative, the Pages tab shows your pages as thumbnails, which when selected, will display that page in your workspace.

Once you've got a page in view, you can use the scrollbars at the right and bottom of the main window to move the page and pasteboard with respect to the main window. As you drag objects to the edge of the screen the scroll bars adjust automatically as the object is kept in view.

To go to a specific page:

1. Choose ⬚ Add/Delete Pages from the context toolbar (shown with Pointer or Rotate Tool selected).

2. On the Page Manager's **Go to Page** tab, type the page number to go to and click **OK**.

- or -

1. Display the **Pages tab** (docked at the bottom of your DrawPlus workspace) by clicking the ▬▬▼▬ button.

2. Click on a thumbnail to jump directly to that page.

To navigate pages:

- Click ◀ **Previous Page**, ▶ **Next Page**, ◀◀ **First Page** or **▶▶** **Last Page** on the HintLine toolbar.

Zooming

The **Hintline** toolbar also allows the user to view and/or edit the page at different levels of detail. You can zoom in/out step-by-step or by a user-defined/preset amount. Panning is also possible.

75%   The **Current Zoom** setting on the toolbar displays the current zoom percentage, with 100% representing an actual-size page. Click over the value, then type to enter any zoom percentage up to 5000% or select a preset zoom from the flyout list (includes fit to **Full Page** or **Page Width**).

To zoom to a particular view:

- Click 🔍 **Zoom Out** or 🔍 **Zoom In** to decrease/increase the current zoom percentage with each click.

- Click 🔍 **Zoom Tool** and drag out a rectangular marquee on the page to define a region to zoom in to. The zoom percentage adjusts accordingly, fitting the designated region into the window. To zoom out, hold down the **Shift** key when dragging or just right-click on the page. You can also pan around a zoomed-in page while the **Ctrl** key is pressed. To zoom to the current selection, choose **Selection** from the **View** menu.

- Click ✋ **Pan Tool** to use a hand cursor to click anywhere on the page and drag to reposition the page in the window.

- Click ⊞ **Fit Page** to adjust the zoom percentage so the entire page area is displayed in the window.

If you're using a wheel mouse, you can scroll the wheel forward or back to move up or down the page, or move horizontally left or right by using the **Shift** key and scrolling together. Try combining the **Ctrl** key and scrolling up or down for immediate in/out zoom control.

Adding and deleting pages

DrawPlus uses the **Page Manager** to add one or more pages before or after a currently selected page; you can even make use of an object "cloning" feature which copies objects from a chosen page.

To add one or more new pages:

1. Select a page from which to add page(s) before/after.

2. Choose ⊡ Add/Delete Pages from the context toolbar (shown with Pointer or Rotate Tool selected)..

3. On the Page Manager's **Insert Page** tab, specify the following:

    - The number of pages to add

    - The page before (or after) the new pages should be added

    - Whether to duplicate a particular page by copying objects from it

4. Click **OK**.

> ★ The document format (as determined in **File>Page Setup...**) will determine whether or not you can add or delete pages. For example, Folded documents have a fixed number of pages.

To delete one or more pages:

1. Choose ⊡ Add/Delete Pages from the context toolbar (shown with Pointer or Rotate Tool selected)..

2. On Page Manager's **Delete Page** tab, specify the following:
    - The number of pages to delete
    - The page after which pages should be deleted

3. Click **OK**.

To duplicate a page:

- On the Insert Page tab, you can specify how many pages to add, and where to add them. Check **Copy objects from page** if you want to duplicate a particular page.

To make a page a background for other pages:

- From the Pages tab, right-click the intended background page and choose **Set as Background** (to undo choose **Unset as background**).

Using design aids

DrawPlus provides a number of tools to assist you as you design. Each is designed to improve stroking lines/brushes, page composition, and focused design on specific areas on the page.

- Rotating your canvas
- Applying the Rule of Thirds
- Using divine proportions
- Isolating an object

Typically the tools can be switched on or off.

Rotating your canvas

Rotating your canvas helps you to maintain natural flow when drawing freeform lines, curves, or brush strokes, where the artist uses the wrist as a pivot (especially when using a pen tablet). If you rotate the canvas by a chosen angle then the drawing becomes easier—taking advantage of the natural arc of the drawing hand.

The above example illustrates how grass-like brush strokes can be added more easily to a canvas once it has been rotated 30°!

To rotate your canvas:

Either:

1. Click [icon] Rotate Canvas on the **Hintline** toolbar (don't click the down arrow).

2. Hover over your workspace until you see the [cursor icon] cursor, then click and drag to rotate the canvas clockwise or anti-clockwise.

3. Once you're happy with the degree of rotation, release the mouse button to reposition the canvas.

- or -

• Click the down arrow on the [icon] Rotate Canvas button (**Hintline** toolbar) and choose a preset angle from the drop-down list.

> You can also select an object and then choose **To Object** from the **Rotate Canvas** drop-down list. The canvas adjusts so that the object is positioned square to the X and Y axes.

To reset your canvas:

• With the button enabled, double-click anywhere on the canvas to reset.

Applying the Rule of Thirds

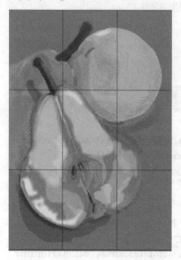

Traditionally a technique used in photography, the **Rule of Thirds** grid can also be applied to your design to help with its composition.

For example, note the way the primary object (pear) is vertically aligned between the top- and bottom-left intersecting points, i.e. under the stalk and core. The secondary object (orange) is located under the opposite intersecting line to offer some balance to the design.

By aligning objects to intersecting horizontal and vertical lines (rather than just centring objects on the page) you can create designs with greater visual interest.

When a grid is applied to your page the displayed context toolbar lets you alter the grid's colour and opacity, and reset or delete the grid. (See online Help.)

> ★ The grid is actually an overlay which appears as an 'Overlay Layer' in the Layers tab. As such you can use the ◉ **Visible** layer control to temporarily show/hide the grid.

To apply a Rule of Thirds grid:

1. From the **Standard** toolbar, click [Overlays ▼] and select **Rule of Thirds** from the drop-down menu. A coloured grid is overlaid over your page.

2. (Optional) For selected objects, drag a corner (or edge) handle to resize the grid; reposition the grid by dragging; rotate by dragging a corner handle. The grid can be manipulated just like an object.

3. Place pictures, frames, or vector objects under any of the intersecting blue lines.

Once applied, the grid stays selected. Clicking away from the grid will deselect it, but it can be reselected at any time (e.g., for repositioning later).

To select the grid:

- From the **Standard** toolbar, click  and choose **Select Rule of Thirds**.

Using divine proportions

Divine proportions in DrawPlus involve overlaying a grid over your design for aesthetic proportioning of design elements. The grid uses the classic golden ratio principle commonly encountered in:

- classic drawings (e.g., da Vinci's Vitruvian Man).

- musical instruments (opposite).

- buildings (Athen's Parthenon).

- modern iconic design (Apple iPod).

> The golden ratio can be understood using the human arm as an example—the ratio (0.618) between instrument's neck and its body.

"Golden" Spirals, Rectangles, and Tangents make up the grid, each differently coloured for easy distinction. Their colours can be changed and each grid component can be hidden from the context toolbar.

To apply a Divine Proportions grid:

1. From the **Standard** toolbar, click 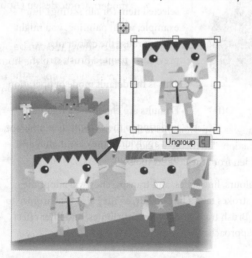 and select **Divine Proportions** from the drop-down menu. The grid is overlaid over your page.

2. (Optional) Resize, rotate, or reposition the grid over your design (or planned design area) by dragging corner or edge handles.

3. Begin drawing, using the guide lines to draw objects proportionately.

To select the grid (once deselected):

- From the **Standard** toolbar, click and choose **Select Divine Proportions**.

Isolating an object

For focused editing, DrawPlus X3 provides the **Solo mode**. This allows you to temporarily isolate selected object(s) on the page that you are currently designing (all unselected objects disappear!). In doing so, you avoid having to move objects to other layers or lock object unnecessarily.

- Select the object, then click [icon] **Solo Mode** on the **Hintline** toolbar. After editing, click the button again to return to normal editing mode.

Updating defaults

When you create new objects in DrawPlus, the way they look depends on the current default settings for that particular type of object. DrawPlus stores defaults separately for (1) lines/shapes (including QuickShapes), (2) artistic text objects, (3) connectors, (4) dimension objects and (5) brushes.

Defaults for shape text (as contained in shapes) are distinct from those for artistic text, and are defined along with other shape defaults (they are subsumed under other shape properties). For any object, default means the properties of the object (line/fill attributes) that will be applied to the next new object (of the same type) you create.

You can adopt two approaches to controlling your defaults according to your preferred way of working, i.e.

[icon] **Synchronize Defaults** (from flyout on **Standard** toolbar)	**On**	Defaults are changed **dynamically** by synchronizing to the colour, style, transparency, or effect of the currently selected item (or tab setting). For example, when painting, you might want to reuse the colour of a previously painted brush stroke.
		This is the default mode of operation.
Synchronize Defaults	**Off**	Defaults are changed by **manually** updating to the current item selection, and apply until they are manually updated again.

Normally, fill and line colours, line styles, and transparency will adopt the former approach. Brush strokes take a line colour, so they also synchronize to the currently set colour. Brush transparency, text attributes, and filter effect defaults adopt the latter approach.

> ★ To see what the current defaults are for a particular object type, simply create a new object of that type.

Although you can switch Synchronize Defaults on or off globally, it is also possible to independently switch on or off attributes which synchronize with, or update to, the currently selected object.

To change which attributes synchronize:

1. Choose **Synchronization Settings...** from the  **Defaults** flyout (**Standard** toolbar) to optionally select attributes (e.g., fill colour, Line colour, Transparency, etc) from which new defaults will be made.

    Synchronize Defaults

    Synchronize Defaults allows you to determine which attributes of selected items will become the defaults for new items.

    - ☑ General
        - ☑ Fill Colour
        - ☑ Line Colour
        - ☑ Line Style
        - ☑ Transparency
    - ☑ Brush
        - ☑ Transparency
    - ☐ Text
        - ☐ Text Fill Colour
        - ☐ Text Attributes
    - ☐ Advanced
        - ☐ Filter Effects

    [OK] [Cancel]

    In the above example, only the last selected object's line and fill colour, line style, and transparency is used as the future default. If you subsequently change these attributes, then the defaults will be updated (synchronized) automatically.

2. Check or uncheck the check boxes to switch on or off the synchronization of defaults for that attribute.

To switch synchronize defaults off (for manual default control):

- Uncheck **Synchronize Defaults** on the [icon] **Defaults** flyout of the **Standard** toolbar.

To set object defaults manually:

1. With **Synchronize Defaults** disabled, create a sample object (the object type matching the set of defaults you're updating: line/shape, artistic text object, connector, or dimension object), and alter it to use the specific properties you plan to use as defaults.

   - or -

   Use an existing object that already has the right properties.

2. Right-click the object and choose **Update Defaults** (or choose **Update Object Defaults** from the **Format** menu).

★ When you update defaults from a shape, all default shape properties, including **shape text** attributes, are reset at the same time.

★ Shape text properties are stored along with other shape defaults, such as line and fill. To avoid altering these settings when updating shape text defaults, create a new sample shape and modify only its text.

Normally, each time you close a document, object default settings are recorded as "master settings" to be used in future documents. To stop DrawPlus from recording the defaults as master settings, choose **Tools>Save Settings...** and uncheck the **Object Defaults** box.

Resetting defaults

A reset of defaults is useful if you feel the need to get back to basics and return to your original default settings.

- Select **Reset Object Defaults** from the [icon] **Defaults** flyout (**Standard** toolbar). With no objects selected, this acts globally, i.e. it resets all objects back to their default settings. With an object(s) selected, it resets only those object types back to their default.

Lines, Curves, and Shapes

4

Selecting one or more objects

Before you can change any object, you need to select it using one of several tools available from the top of the **Drawing** toolbar.

 Pointer Tool
Click to use the **Pointer Tool** to select, move, copy, resize, or rotate objects.

 Rotate Tool
Click to use the **Rotate Tool** to exclusively rotate an object around a centre of rotation. You can also use the Rotate Tool to move or copy objects.

 Node Tool
Click to use the **Node Tool** to manipulate the shape of objects, or move or copy objects.

To select an object:

- Click on the object using one of the tools shown above. For the Pointer and Rotate Tools, small "handles" appear around the object indicating selection.

For the Node Tool, editable nodes are displayed for lines—sliding handles are additionally shown for adjustment of QuickShapes and text. If objects overlap, click repeatedly (without double-clicking) until the desired object is selected.

> ★ If you select an image with areas of transparency, you'll be able to manipulate the image's outline, i.e. convert to curves, apply line properties, effects, etc.

Selecting multiple objects

It is also possible to select more than one object, making a **multiple selection** that you can manipulate as if it were one object, or turn into a grouped object.

To select more than one object (multiple selection):

1. Choose the Pointer, Rotate or Node Tool.

2. Click in a blank area of the page and drag a "marquee" box around the objects you want to select.

Release the mouse button. All of the objects within the marquee box are selected and one selection box, with handles, appears around the objects. To deselect, click in a blank area of the page.

- or -

1. Click on the first object for selection.

2. Press the **Shift** key down then click on a second object.

3. Continue selecting other objects to build up your multiple selection. Handles (or a bounding box, depending on the tool) appear around the multiple selection.

To select all objects on the page:

- Choose **Select All** from the **Edit** menu.

To add or remove an object from a multiple selection:

- Hold down the **Shift** key and click the object to be added or removed.

Selection using a lasso

For more detailed multiple object selection, using a fixed marquee or **Shift**-select may be too inflexible. Instead, you can draw an irregular-shaped lasso around one or more objects in a complex design.

To select using a lasso:

1. Choose the Pointer or Rotate Tool.

2. With the **Alt** key pressed, draw a "lasso" around the objects you want to select.

3. Release the mouse button. All of the objects within the lasso region are selected.

💡 If attempting to lasso grouped objects remember to ungroup them first.

Drawing lines and shapes

Lines can be either straight or curved. They have properties like **colour** and **weight** (thickness). When a line (or series of line segments) forms a complete, enclosed outline, it becomes a new **closed** object called a **shape**. Because shapes have an interior region that can be filled (for example, with a solid colour or a bitmap), they have **fill properties** as well as **line properties**.

Choose one of the line tools shown below from the **Drawing** toolbar.

 The **Pencil Tool** is used to sketch freeform lines.

 The **Straight Line Tool** is used to draw straight lines.

 The **Pen Tool** is used for drawing complex, combination curves and shapes in a highly controlled way by using a series of "connect the dots" mouse clicks.

As soon as you draw a line, or choose one of the line tools when a line is selected, you'll see the line's **nodes** appear. Nodes show the end points of each segment in the line. Curved lines usually have many nodes; straight lines have only two.

Drawing lines

To draw a freeform line:

1. Choose the **Pencil Tool** from the **Drawing** toolbar.

2. Click once, then drag across the page, drawing a line as you go. The line appears immediately and follows your mouse movements.

3. To end the line, release the mouse button. The line will automatically smooth out using a minimal number of nodes. Note the dots indicating its nodes—at the two ends, and at each point where two line segments come together.

4. (optional) To set the degree of smoothing to be applied to the line (and subsequent lines), set the **Smoothness** value on the context toolbar above your workspace.

Click its right arrow to display a slider—drag right, then left. You'll see your drawn line—still selected—smooth out (with fewer nodes) as you drag right, and become more jagged (with more nodes) as you drag left. For the smoothest curves the next time you draw a freeform line, leave the sliding arrow towards the right of the slider.

To draw a straight line:

1. Click the  **Straight Line Tool** from the **Drawing** toolbar's Line Tools flyout.

2. Click where you want the line to start, and drag to another point while holding down the mouse button, then release the mouse button. The straight line appears immediately.

> To constrain the angle of the straight line to 15° increments, hold down the **Shift** key down as you drag. (This is an easy way to make exactly vertical or horizontal lines.)

Any kind of open line (that is, one that hasn't been closed to create a shape) can be extended, and you can use any of the three line tools to do so. Use the Pointer Tool and then the line's drawing tool to resize or reshape lines once you've drawn them.

To extend a line:

1.   Move the cursor over either of the end nodes, a small + cursor will appear. Click at that location.

2.   The line that you drag out will be a continuation of the existing line, as a new line segment.

To draw a curved line:

1.   Choose the 🖋 **Pen Tool** from the **Drawing** toolbar.

2.   ⌢ ⌃ From the displayed context toolbar, choose to create your drawn segments in **Smooth joins** or **Sharp joins** creation mode. By default, you'll be in **Smooth joins** mode (i.e., drawing Bézier curves segment-by-segment). Sharp joins would create a zig-zag line without curving through nodes.

3.   Click where you want the line to start (**1**).

4.   Click again for a new node and drag out a pair of **control handles** which orbit the node (**2**). (Control handles act like "magnets," pulling the curve into shape. The distance between handles determines the depth of the resulting curved line.) Release the mouse button to create your curve segment (**3**).

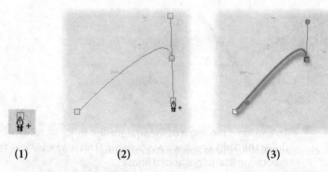

(**1**)   (**2**)   (**3**)

5.   To extend an existing line, click beyond the end of your current curve to create a new node (thus creating another curve segment). Normally, curve segments end in a symmetric (evenly rounded) corner (**4**), with control handles locked together.

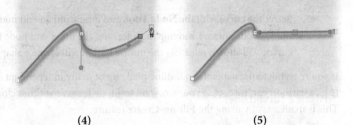

(4)   (5)

6. However, you can press the **Alt** key while drawing the segment to define a "cusp" or sharp corner (**5**). This locks the control handle on the last created node. For more on line corners, see Changing nodes and line segments.

7. To end the line, press **Esc** or choose a different tool.

Drawing shapes

You can make a shape by closing a curve—extending a freeform line or a segmented straight line back to its starting point. Shapes have an interior which is filled with the current **default fill** (see Setting fill properties on p. 143) when the shape is closed.

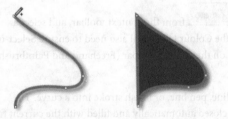

To close an existing curve (with a straight line):

1. Select the curve with the Node Tool, Pencil or Pen Tool.

2. Click **Close Curve** on the context toolbar. A Straight segment appears, closing the curve.

To close a curve (without new segment):

- Select the curve with the **Node Tool**, and drag from an end node (note the ▷ Node cursor), moving the line, onto the other end node (a Close cursor will show); releasing the mouse button will create a shape.

If you're trying to draw a cartoon outline made up of many independent curves (e.g., a cartoon ear, rose, etc.) you may want to fill each curve without closing it. This is made easy by using the **Fill-on-Create** feature.

To fill an unclosed curve automatically:

- Select the Pencil Tool, Pen Tool, or Paintbrush Tool.

- Enable ⟨ Fill-on-Create from the context toolbar, and select a suitable fill from the Colour tab. You'll also need to ensure **Select-on-Create** is enabled on the context toolbar (Freehand and Paintbrush tools only).

- Draw a freeform line, pen line, or brush stroke into a curve. The resulting curve is closed automatically and filled with the current fill colour.

Editing lines and shapes

To edit lines or shapes, you can manipulate their segments and/or nodes, allowing you to:

- Redraw part of a curve

- Reshape a line (or curve)

- Simplify a line (remove nodes)

- Enhance a line (add nodes)

- Change the type of node or line segment

- Convert to straight line segments

- Adjust a shape

- Join two lines together

Redrawing part of a curve

With the **Pencil Tool**, it's easy to redraw any portion of a curve.

To redraw part of a selected curve:

1. Select the line, then the  **Pencil Tool**. Hover the displayed cursor on the line where you want to begin redrawing. The cursor changes to indicate you can begin drawing.

2.   Click on the line, and a new node appears.

3.   Keep the mouse button down and drag to draw a new line section, connecting it back to another point on the original line. Again, the cursor changes to include a curve when you're close enough to the line to make a connection. When you release the mouse button, the original portion is replaced by the newly drawn portion.

Reshaping a line

The main tool for editing lines and shapes is the **Node Tool**. In general, you first use the **Node Tool** to select one or more nodes on the object, then use the buttons on the tool's supporting context toolbar.

To reshape a curved line:

1.   Click the ⧨ **Node Tool** on the **Drawing** toolbar.

2.   Select any curved line on your page. The line's nodes appear, and the context toolbar also pops up.

3.   Hover over a segment and drag the segment to form a new curve shape.

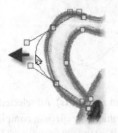

- or -

Select nodes and drag. Selection can be by one of the following methods:

  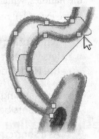

Hover over a single node and click to select the node. **Shift**-click for multiple nodes.	drag out a marquee to select multiple neighbouring nodes	drag out a lasso (with **Alt** key pressed) to select multiple nodes otherwise difficult to select via a marquee.

Once selected, a node becomes highlighted and **control handles** for the adjacent line segment(s) will appear.

Note that each segment in the line has a control handle at either end, so when you select an **end node** or **interior node**, indicated below, you'll see either a control handle on each selected end node (one segment) or a pair of handles at a selected interior node (two segments), respectively, i.e.

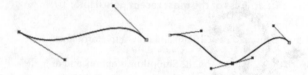

4. Drag any selected node to reshape adjacent segment(s). All selected nodes move in the same direction, so you can reshape the curve in complex ways by selecting specific nodes. **Shift**-drag to constrain the movement to horizontal or vertical.

5. Drag one or more control handles to produce very precise changes in the curvature of the line on either side of a node. You can shorten or lengthen the handles, which changes the depth of the **curve** (that is, how far out the curve extends), or alter the handle angle, which changes the curve's **slope**.

> ★ When using the Pen Tool, pressing the **Ctrl** key while clicking a node lets you edit the curve directly. This saves having to jump back to the Node Tool. You can't edit multiple nodes simultaneously.
>
> ★ By changing the type of node you can change how the adjacent segments behave.
>
> ★ As a shortcut when selecting nodes, you can press **Tab** or **Shift-Tab** to select the next or previous node along the line (following the order in which nodes were created).

Simplifying or enhancing a line

The more nodes there are on a line or shape, the more control over its shape you have. The fewer nodes there are, the simpler (smoother) the line or shape. You can adjust the **Smoothness** to refine the curve most recently drawn (as long as the line is still selected). It is also possible to add or delete nodes to simplify or enhance curves, and even clean curves (removing unnecessary nodes automatically).

To adjust the smoothness of the most recent pencil line:

1. Choose the **Pencil Tool** and draw a freeform line.

2. Click the right arrow on the **Smoothness** option and drag the displayed slider left to increase the number of nodes (you can also add absolute values into the input box).

3. To make the curve less complex, i.e. smoother, drag the slider right to decrease the number of nodes.

To add or delete a node:

- To **add a node**, click along a line segment with the Node Tool or Pen Tool to add a new node at that point. The new node will be created and will be selected (complete with attractor nodes as necessary).

- To **delete a node**, select the line with the Node Tool then the node itself and click the **Delete Node** button on the context toolbar (or press the **Delete** key). The node will be deleted, along with any associated attractor nodes, and the line or shape will jump to its new shape. With the Pen Tool selected, you can also delete a node by clicking on it.

You can also use the Node Tool to reposition the nodes, and reshape the line or shape, by dragging on the new handles.

Changing nodes and line segments

Each segment in a line has a control handle at either end, so at each interior or "corner" node (where two segments join) you'll see a pair of handles. The behaviour of these handles—and thus the curvature of the segments to either side—depends on whether the node is set to be **sharp**, **smooth**, **symmetric**, or **smart**. You can quickly identify a node's type by selecting it and seeing which button is selected in the displayed context toolbar. Each type's control handles behave differently as illustrated below.

To change one or more nodes to a different type:

1. Select the object with the **Node Tool**, followed by the node(s) you want to change.

2. Click one of the node buttons (described below) on the displayed context toolbar.

A **Sharp Corner** means that the line segments to either side of the node are completely independent so that the corner can be quite pointed.

A **Smooth Corner** means that the slope of the line is the same on both sides of the node, but the depth of the two joined segments can be different.

At a **Symmetric Corner**, nodes join line segments with the same slope and depth on both sides of the node. **Note:** Normally, Custom segments you draw with the Pen Tool end in a symmetric corner.

Smart Corner nodes automatically determine slope and depth for a rounded, best-fitting curve. If you attempt to adjust a smart corner's handles, it reverts to a symmetric corner. You can always reset the node to smart—but to maintain smart nodes, be careful what you click on!

You can also use the context toolbar to define a line segment as either straight or curved.

To change a line segment from straight to curved, or vice versa:

1. With the **Node Tool**, select the leading node of the line segment (the node nearer the start of the line).

2. Then, either:

    - To make a line segment straight, click Straighten Line on the context toolbar. The selected segment immediately jumps to a straight line.

      - or -

    - To make a line segment curved, click one of the node buttons on the context toolbar: Sharp Corner, Smooth Corner, Symmetric Corner, or Smart Corner. You can then adjust the curvature of the newly created curved segment.

To convert to straight lines:

1. With the Node Tool, select the curve.

2. From the context toolbar, choose **Convert to Straight Lines**. The curve segments are replaced by straight line segments throughout the line.

Adjusting a shape

As described on p. 59, you can easily turn a curve into a shape by connecting its end nodes. You can go the other way, too—break open a shape in order to add one or more line segments.

To break open a line or shape:

1. With the **Node Tool**, select the node on the closed curve where you want the break to occur.

2. Click **Break Curve** on the context toolbar so that the line will separate. A shape will become a line, with the selected node split into two nodes, one at each end of the new line.

3. You can now use the Node Tool to reposition the nodes and reshape the line by dragging on the handles.

> ★ When you first break a curve the two nodes are in exactly the same location and so the curve may still look as if it is connected. If you drag one of the red node ends away you will quickly see the separation.

Joining lines together

You can connect any two straight or curved lines to form a new line.

To join two lines together:

1. Select both lines by **Shift**-clicking with any selection tool.

2. Choose **Join Curves** from the **Tools** menu. The end control node of one line is connected with the start control node of the other.

Using QuickShapes

QuickShapes are pre-designed objects that you can instantly add to your page, then adjust and vary using **control handles**. QuickShapes are added from a flyout containing a wide variety of commonly used shapes, including boxes, arrows, hearts, spirals and other useful symbols.

To create a QuickShape:

1. Click the down arrow on the [ ] **QuickShape** button on the **Drawing** toolbar, then select a shape from the flyout. The button takes on the icon of the shape you selected.

2. At your chosen cursor position, either:

   - Double-click to place a default-sized QuickShape.

     - or -

- Click and drag on the page to draw out your QuickShape to a chosen size (use the Shift key to lock the aspect ratio; the Ctrl key to scale from its centre point; or both together).

New QuickShapes adopt the currently set line and fill in DrawPlus.

All QuickShapes can be positioned, resized, rotated, and filled. What's more, you can "morph" their designs. For example, dragging the handles on a Quick Polygon will change the number of sides to make a triangle, pentagon, hexagon, or other polygon.

To adjust the appearance of a QuickShape:

1. Click on the QuickShape to reveal sliding handles around the shape. These are distinct from the "inner" selection handles. Different QuickShapes have different handles.

2. Drag any handle to change the appearance of the QuickShape.

For example, by dragging the top sliding handle to the right on the pentagon below will quickly produce an octagon:

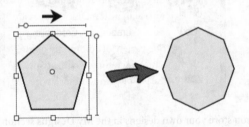

You can also use the Line tab and Swatch tab to alter any object's line/fill properties after it has been drawn.

Using the Gallery

The Studio's Gallery tab contains pre-built design objects and elements you'd like to reuse in different drawings. Arts and Crafts, Cartoons, Connecting Symbols (for family trees, electronics, and computers), Layout Symbols (for garden and home), and ShapeArt are all folders under which various categories (or further sub-folders) are stored. When you install the DrawPlus X3 Resource CD the Gallery tab also includes further categories (Curriculum and Business) for your use.

The Gallery tab has two parts: (1) an upper **Folder/Categories** drop-down menu and (2) a lower **Designs** window where you can select and drag a copy of the design onto your page.

The Gallery tab also lets you store your own designs in the **My Designs** section if you would like to reuse them—the design is made available in any DrawPlus document. You can add and delete your items within each category, with the option of naming elements to facilitate rapid retrieval.

New design categories can be added to any design folder which exists under the user's **My Designs** category (but not under any read-only pre-defined category). You can rename or delete any design by right-clicking on the design thumbnail.

To use a design from the Gallery:

- Drag any preset design directly onto the page. The Gallery retains a copy of the design until you expressly delete it. You can modify, then drag the design back into your own custom category.

To view your Gallery:

- Click the Studio's **Gallery** tab.

- Select a folder or category from the drop-down menu. The items from the folder's first listed category are displayed by default.

To add, delete, or rename design folder (or category):

1. Right-click in the drop-down menu and choose **Add Folder...** (or **Add Category...**, **Delete Category/Folder**, or **Rename Category/Folder...**.

2. For adding and renaming, use the dialog to enter and/or confirm your change.

To add, delete, or rename design categories:

1. Right-click in the Categories list and choose **Add Category...**, **Delete Category/Folder**, or **Rename Category/Folder...**.

2. For adding and renaming, use the dialog to enter and/or confirm your change.

To copy an object into the Gallery:

1. Display the Gallery tab's **My Designs** category (or sub-category of that) where you want to store the copy.

2. Drag the object from the page and drop it onto the gallery.

3. You'll be prompted to type a name for the design. (You can name or rename the design later, if you wish.) By default, unnamed designs are labeled as "Untitled."

4. A thumbnail of the design appears in the gallery, labelled with its name.

To delete or rename a design:

- Right-click its gallery thumbnail and choose **Delete Design...** or **Rename Design...** from the submenu.

Converting a shape to editable curves

The conversion of QuickShapes to curves provides you with a starting point for your own shapes, whereas converting text to curves is one way of incorporating editable letter-based shapes into designs.

To convert an object into curves:

1. Select your QuickShape or text object.

2. Click ![icon] **Convert to Curves** on the Arrange tab.

3. Edit the curve outline using the Node Tool.

However they were created, all converted objects behave in a similar manner. For example, you can create some text with the Artistic Text Tool, convert it to curves, then use the Node Tool to edit the curves that make up the letters, just as if you had drawn the letter shapes by hand using the line tools.

> The conversion process loses all of the special properties inherent in QuickShapes and text.

Check **Clean Curves** in **Tools>Options>General** to automatically reduce the number of nodes during convert to curve operations—this makes editing a little easier!

Applying perspective

The **Perspective Tool**, like the adjacent Envelope Tool, produces an overall shape distortion. But while the Envelope effect stretches the object as if it were printed on a rubber sheet, perspective gives you the visual impression of a flat surface being tilted (or skewed) in space, with an exaggerated front/back size differential.

To apply a perspective effect:

1. Select an object and click  **Perspective Tool** on the **Drawing** toolbar. The Node Tool becomes the active tool and an adjustment slider appears above the object.

2. Drag the ✛ "3D" cursor over the selected object or drag the special adjustment slider handle left or right to see it respond by tilting in all sorts of orientations. Use Undo if you're not happy with a particular adjustment.

    - or -

    From the context toolbar, select an item from the [▢ Perspective Presets ▼] flyout closest to the effect you're after. The first item, **User Defined perspective**, retrieves the last drawn custom perspective shape used in your current DrawPlus session. You can still use the cursor and handles for adjusting perspective.

Applying envelopes

An envelope distortion is one that you can apply to any object to change its shape without having to edit its nodes. You can use envelopes to bend text into a wave, arch, trapezoid, or just about any other shape. You can edit envelopes into custom shapes and apply them to other objects for corresponding effects.

With the **Envelope Tool**, an object's nodes can be moved in order to create custom envelopes or to allow preset envelopes to be applied to the selected object. The displayed context toolbar, shown while the tool is active, offers various options to customize the envelope—envelope shape, line colour, weight, and style can all be altered. It also lets you pick from a range of pre-defined envelopes of various shapes, remove the selected object's envelope or apply curve adjustments on the envelope's boundary.

To apply an envelope:

1. Select the object(s) you want to be enveloped.

2. Click ⊠ **Envelope Tool** on the **Drawing** toolbar.

3. From the context toolbar, select a preset from the ⊠ Preset Envelopes ▾ flyout. The first item, User Defined envelope, retrieves the last drawn custom envelope shape used in your current DrawPlus session.

To remove an envelope:

1. Select the envelope with the **Envelope Tool**.

2. Click ⊠ Remove Envelope from the Envelope context toolbar.

To create/edit your own envelope:

You can create an envelope or edit any of the preset envelopes once they have been applied by dragging the nodes and handles accordingly.

- Select the object(s) with the **Envelope Tool**. DrawPlus automatically selects the Node tool when an envelope is applied. The Node Tool along with the displayed curve buttons on the Envelope context toolbar lets you reshape the envelope by dragging its corner nodes and attractor nodes, as when editing curved lines. (To review these concepts, see Editing lines and shapes on p. 61.) The only difference is that you cannot add or delete corner nodes to an envelope. Envelopes always have exactly four line segments, one on each side.

Connectors

Connectors are special lines that you can anchor to objects, where they remain attached even if one or both objects are moved or resized. Using connectors, you can easily create dynamic diagrams and charts that show relationships, such as family trees, organization charts, and flow charts. If you need to rearrange the elements, the connections are preserved.

Each DrawPlus object has default connection points, displayed whenever you select one of the connector tools and hover over the object. These default points (which can't be moved or deleted) are called **Auto Select** points.

To create a connection:

1. Select 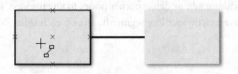 **Connector Tool** on the Line Tools flyout (**Drawing** toolbar). Hover over an object so that default **Auto Select connection points** become visible, e.g. as on the left Quick Rectangle:

2. From the context toolbar, select  **Direct Connector Tool**.

3. Click the connection point on the right edge midpoint of the left shape. Drag to the right and release the mouse button when the pointer is over the connection point on the left edge midpoint of the right shape. (You'll see a box appear around the point when a connection is imminent.) A direct connector will appear between the two connection points.

4. Select the right-hand shape and drag to a new position with the Pointer Tool; the connection points vanish, but the connector remains. The connector follows!

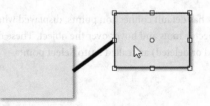

Connector types

The **Connector Tool**, when selected, offers various types of connector tool on the Connectors context toolbar situated above the workspace.

 Choose the **Direct Connector Tool** to draw a single, straight-line connector between any two connection points.

 Choose the **Right Angle Connector Tool** for a connector with only vertical and horizontal segments (the connector shape is made up of right angles)—for example, if you're creating a flow chart, organization chart, or tree diagram.

Choose the **Auto Connector Tool** for an adaptable connector that intelligently adjusts its shape to route around "obstructive" objects. Unlike the other connectors, Auto connectors automatically form "bridges" when crossing each other, so they're perfect for complex diagrams with interwoven pathways.

💡 The context toolbar is also used to adjust a connector's line weight, line end, colour and style.

💡 You can create your own additional custom connection points, created with the Connection Point Tool, which can be placed anywhere on an object.

Using Brushes

Using Brushes

Selecting brushes

DrawPlus supports a wide range of brushes, all capable of producing:

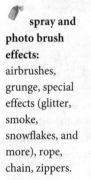 **natural brush effects**: natural media (charcoal, pastel, pen, pencil, paint, watercolour) or photo brushes (stitching).

spray and photo brush effects: airbrushes, grunge, special effects (glitter, smoke, snowflakes, and more), rope, chain, zippers.

Painting inherits the principles of Drawing lines and shapes (see p. 55). The drawing freedom of the Pencil Tool is adapted for brushwork using the dedicated **Paintbrush Tool**. You can pick up colour for your brushes as you would for other object, by simply selecting the Paintbrush Tool, choosing your **brush type** from the Brushes tab and picking a brush colour from the Colour or Swatch tab.

> Brushes based on bitmaps cannot be recoloured.

The Brushes tab lets you **select** a brush type from a range of natural (opposite), spray or photo-based categories. You can also view brushes currently being used in your document, and edit brushes or create your own brushes (see online Help).

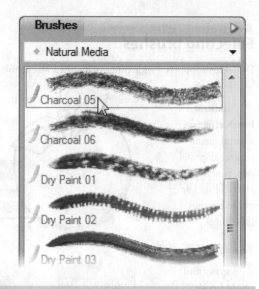

> Natural and spray brush types are indicated by <img/> and <img/> symbols, respectively.

To make sense of all the brush types available to the user, the preset brushes are stored under a series of pre-defined categories under the name **Global**—the brushes are available to all DrawPlus documents currently open. The **Document** category shows the brush types currently in use in the DrawPlus drawing and is used to "bookmark" brushes for easy reuse in the future.

At some point, you may want to edit, copy or create your own natural stroke or spray brush type. See online Help.

Brush strokes can be applied directly to the page by using your mouse or tablet; the latter method is ideally suited for applying customizable pressure-sensitive strokes to your drawing. However, painting with the mouse still provides a viable alternative to the tablet. Pressure sensitivity is simulated by use of ready-made customizable pressure profile presets.

Applying brush strokes

The 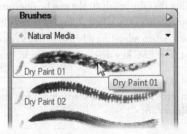 **Paintbrush Tool** is used exclusively to apply brush strokes to the page. The tool is used in conjunction with the Brushes tab, and a supporting context toolbar.

To apply a brush stroke:

1. Select the **Paintbrush Tool** from the **Drawing** toolbar.

2. Display the Brushes tab and choose a brush from a category (use the drop-down list for different categories).

3. Select a **Colour**, **Width**, or **Opacity** from the Brush context toolbar.

> Brushes based on bitmaps cannot be recoloured.

4. (Optional) From the context toolbar, adjust **Smoothness** (to set how smooth your stroke is applied) via a slider.

5. (Optional) Enable [● Select-on-Create] to leave the brush stroke selected on the page or, if disabled, leaves it deselected.

6. (Optional) Enable [● Fill-on-Create] to fill the unclosed curve produced with the brush stroke with a default fill colour.

7. With the ✍ brush cursor drag a brush stroke across your page.

After this first brush stroke, there are two ways in which you are likely to paint subsequently, depending on the extent to which you plan to edit brush strokes as you go. To assist you, the **Select on Create** button on the Brushes context toolbar can be used:

- **Edit then Paint**. With the button disabled, the brush stroke is laid down and is immediately deselected. The stroke needs to be reselected to perform any editing. Use when you're happy to set all the brush properties (colour, brush type, width, etc) before painting (as above), especially if you intend to paint repeatedly with the same brush stroke.

- **Paint and Edit**. With the button enabled, a painted brush stroke will remain selected, meaning that the brush stroke can be fine-tuned via the context toolbar immediately. Use when changing your brush properties frequently, e.g. when adjusting a brush stroke's colour, width, opacity or shape. The **ESC** key deselects the current brush stroke.

🖐 Trouble applying colour to brush strokes? Remember to select the line swatch on the **Colour** tab.

Setting Brush Defaults

See Updating defaults on p. 47.

Editing brush strokes

It's possible to alter any previously draw brush stroke with respect to its properties, brush type, and shape.

To change brush stroke properties:

- Use the Brushes context toolbar to adjust the properties of a drawn brush stroke once applied to your page.

To change brush stroke type:

1. Select the brush stroke.

2. Go to the Brushes tab and select firstly a brush category then a brush type from the displayed gallery. The brush stroke adopts the newly chosen brush.

> Brush types currently applied to your brush strokes are handily listed in the Document folder of the Brushes tab.

To change the shape of your brush stroke:

A brush stroke possesses very similar characteristics to a plain line. Any brush stroke can therefore be edited, extended, or redrawn with the **Node Tool** (**Drawing** toolbar) just as for a straight or curved line (see Editing lines and shapes on p. 61). Use for fine-tuning your brush strokes after application.

Pressure sensitivity

Along with a brush's natural characteristics (its bristles, shape, and size), pressure sensitivity also plays a major part in how a brush is applied to your page. The extent to which a brush is applied is at the heart of an artist's creative ability. A heavily applied brush could help to convey strong imagery (e.g., moods), whereas a brush applied more lightly may indicate a more subtle effect.

In DrawPlus's world we apply pressure by using a pressure-sensitive device (a tablet and pen) and control how that pressure affects your brush stroke in DrawPlus's Pressure tab. This tab is used to apply different pressure profile presets, create your own profiles from scratch and adjusts how the brush's width and transparency changes as it responds to pressure. The maximum and minimum pressure can also be controlled via the tab—your brush strokes can appear more subtle or striking as a result.

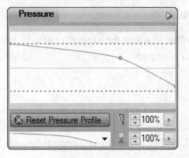

The pressure chart may appear a little daunting at first! It becomes a lot clearer if you imagine the chart when it is superimposed over the brush itself —it represents one half of a brush stroke along its entire length exactly. Of course, the same profile shape will be mirrored on the lower half of the stroke.

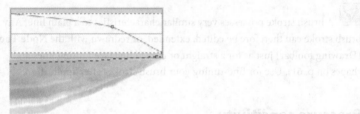

To apply a pressure profile:

1. Expand the Pressure tab at the bottom right of your screen, and choose a pressure profile from the drop-down menu.

    The pressure chart updates to reflect the chosen profile.

2. Apply a brush stroke to the page. This will adopt the chosen pressure profile.

The profile is maintained until you reset it or pick another profile from the preset list.

To create a new pressure profile:

1. Click ⊗ Reset Pressure Profile . This sets the pressure chart back to default.

2. A turquoise line runs along the maximum pressure line at the top of the chart. Click on this line (the cursor changes) and drag downwards, moving the displayed red node into your chosen position. You now have a blue curve which represents the pressure profile.

3. Repeat the process for the number of nodes that you want to add to make up the profile.

> ★ Edit an existing pressure profile from the preset drop-down menu to create profiles quickly.

You can then save the current pressure settings to your own saved pressure profile—this allows you to store and reapply your settings at any point in the future.

To save a new pressure profile:

*   Click on the ▷ **Tab Menu** button and select **Add Pressure Profile.**

Your new profile is automatically added to the bottom of the pressure profile preset drop-down list.

To delete a pressure profile:

1. Click on the ▷ **Tab Menu** button and select **Manage Pressure Profiles...**.

2. In the dialog, select the pressure profile for deletion and click the **Delete** button.

Altering brush width and opacity with pressure

For subtle brush pressure control, DrawPlus can vary the extent to which pen pressure can alter a brush's original width and opacity. This is expressed as a percentage of the original brush **Width** and **Opacity** values shown in the Brushes context toolbar. Imagine the end of your brush stroke tapering off or getting fainter as it lifts off the page—the concept is simple!

You can set the degree to which width and opacity changes either independently or in combination. Let's look at some examples... based on a **Default** brush called "Circle". The example doesn't use a natural media texture so the concept is illustrated more clearly. We'll use a pressure profile available from the preset drop-down menu for all examples.

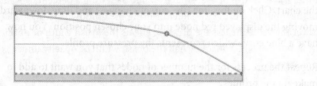

Here's how the degree of width/opacity changes the brush stroke appearance.

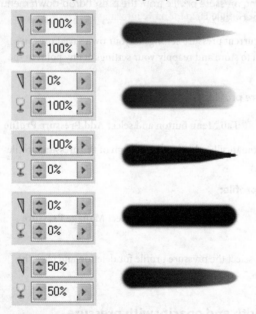

The first example shows the default behaviour when brush pressure is applied.

These settings are adjusted independently and are not stored with the pressure profiles.

To adjust brush width or opacity with pressure:

1. Select a previously drawn brush.

2. In the Pressure tab, pick a pressure profile from the drop-down menu.

3. Enter a **Width** or **Opacity** value by setting a percentage value in the input box, using the slider or using the up/down arrows. The lower the value the less the pressure effects the brush width or opacity, i.e. a value of 50% will apply half the brush width or opacity under pressure.

You can set the pressure variance, i.e. the degree to which you apply brush pressure, via the Pressure tab by increasing/decreasing the lower or upper limits of the pressure chart. (See online Help for more information).

Working with Text

Working with Text

Entering text

You can create different types of text in DrawPlus, i.e. **Artistic Text**, **Frame Text**, or **Shape Text**, all directly on the page.

Morbi nisl eros,
dignissim nec, malesuada
et, convallis quis, augue.
Vestibulum ante ipsum
primis in faucibus orci
luctus et ultrices posuere
cubilia Curae; Proin

...Lorem   ipsum....
dolor sit amet,
consectetuer adipiscing
elit. "Suspendisse erat
massa, dapibus at,."

| Artistic Text | Frame Text | Shape Text |

It's easy to edit the text once it's created, by retyping it or altering properties like font, style, and point size.

In general, artistic text (as an independent object) is better suited to decorative or fancy typographic design, frame text is intended for presenting text passages in more traditional square or rectangular shaped blocks; shape text lends itself so well to blocks of body text where shape and flow contribute to the overall layout.

Artistic text behaves more independently than Shape and Frame Text and its individual letters can be stretched, rotated, sheared, enveloped, and combined with other objects. Shape text lacks a line property, but it conforms to the containing shape, and you can achieve unique text flow effects by varying the container's properties. (See Fitting text to frames and shapes for details.)

Default settings (p. 47) are stored separately for artistic text and frame text.

To enter new artistic text:

1. Select **A** **Artistic Text** on the **Drawing** toolbar's Text flyout.

2. To create **artistic text** at the current default point size, click where you want to start the text.

    - or -

For artistic text that will be automatically sized into an area, click and drag out the area to the desired size.

3. To set text attributes (font, size, etc.) before you start typing, make selections on the Text context toolbar. For colour, set the Line/Fill swatches on the Studio's Colour or Swatch tab.

4. Start typing.

To create frame text:

1. Select ![icon] **Frame Text** on the **Drawing** toolbar's Text flyout.

2. From the positioned cursor, either:

    -   Double-click on the page or pasteboard to create a new frame at a default size.

        - or -

    -   Drag out a frame to your desired frame dimension.

3. (Optional) Set text and colour attributes as for artistic text before you start typing.

4. Start typing within the frame.

To enter new shape text:

1. Create a QuickShape either from the QuickShape flyout or by closing a drawn line.

2. With a shape still selected, just start typing.

For existing shapes without shape text, select the shape, then click in its centre, then start typing.

Working with Unicode text

On occasion, you may wish to import text in a foreign language, e.g. you may want to include a foreign quote in its original language. To work outside the standard ASCII character set, DrawPlus allows Unicode characters to be pasted (using **Edit>Paste Special...**) from the clipboard into your drawing.

To retain formatting, use "*Formatted Text (RTF)*" or for plain text use "*Unformatted Unicode Text*". For the latter, if your imported text appears as blocks instead, remember to apply a Unicode font such as Arial Unicode MS to fix the formatting.

Editing text

Once you've entered either **artistic**, **frame** or **shape text** (see Entering text on p. 93), you can retype it and/or format its character attributes (font, point size, bold/italic/underline, etc.), paragraph properties, and text flow. Text objects have graphic properties, too: artistic text behaves like an independent graphic object (it can be scaled), while shape or frame text conforms to its container or frame.

Artistic text, text frames, and shapes containing text can all be rotated, skewed, moved, and copied. You can also apply line and fill colour independently, brush strokes/edges, or apply opacity and transparency effects, for interesting text effects.

Colour can be applied to selected text as a solid, gradient or bitmap fill—for a solid fill, simply select one or more characters and apply a solid colour from the Studio's Colour tab (ensuring the fill swatch is set) or the Character dialog. See Setting fill properties on p. 143.

For a gradient or bitmap fill, use the Studio's Swatch tab. See p. 155 or p. 159, respectively.

Similarly, opacity is applied from the Colour tab (see p. 162); gradient and bitmap transparency from the Transparency tab.

Retyping text

You can either retype artistic, frame or shape text directly on the page, or use the Edit Text window—great for managing large amounts of text (overflowed shape text or otherwise) in a simple word processing environment.

To retype text on the page:

1.   Select the object and then select **A** **Artistic Text** (from the **Drawing** toolbar's Text flyout), in either order.

2.   Type new text at the selection point or drag to select text, then type to replace it. To cut, copy, and paste, use the toolbar buttons or standard Windows keyboard shortcuts.

To create a new line:

*   At the position you want to start a new line, press the **Enter** key.

Formatting text

You can change text formatting (character, paragraph, bullets/numbering and text flow properties) either directly on the page or via the Edit Text window.

In addition, artistic text characters have line properties, expanding their creative possibilities.

To format selected text on the page:

1.   Use the **Pointer Tool** to select the text you want to change.

     Alternatively, drag select on any text with **A** **Artistic Text** (from the **Drawing** toolbar's Text flyout).

2.   Use the Text context toolbar to change text properties (font, point size, bold/italic/underline, text alignment, bullets and numbering, levels, and text fitting).

     - or -

     Choose **Character...**, **Paragraph...**, **Tabs...**, **Bullets and Numbering...**, or **Text Flow...** from the **Format** menu (or the right-click menu).

★ The ▽ **Node Tool** can be used for special adjustments on artistic text.

★ For greater control over the shape of the artistic text characters, try converting the artistic text to **curves**. As curves, you can position every character individually and even edit the character shapes, exactly as if you had drawn the character shapes by hand using the line tools. For details, see Converting a shape to editable curves on p. 72.

Fitting text to frames and shapes

Text overflow

If there's too much text to fit into a text frame or shape, the Overflow 🄰 button appears beneath the shape; DrawPlus stores the overflowing text in an invisible overflow area.

To make all the text fit you might edit the story down to allow text to fit in the frame or shape. However, scaling the text to fit may be preferable where you can scale the shape or frame text size so it fits exactly into the available frame.

To scale the frame or shape text:

- Click Overflow 🄰 to **autofit** the frame or shape text to its container. AutoFit first applies small point size changes, then small leading changes, then adjustments to the paragraph space below value, until the text fits. Other settings are not affected.

 - or -

- Use 🔳 **Autofit** on the Text context toolbar.

For incremental scaling, use the ⊞ **Enlarge Text** or ⊞ **Shrink Text** buttons on the same toolbar.

Positioning

- **Vertical alignment** (right-click **Text>Text Flow...**) moves existing text to the Top, Bottom, or Centre of the container (alternatively you can justify text vertically). The setting anchors a particular part of the object—for example, a "Top" setting anchors the top line and forces new text to come in below, while a "Bottom" setting anchors the bottom (most recent) line and pushes previous lines up as you type new lines.

- To add white space around your text, you can indent text from the frame or shape edge via right-click **Text>Text Flow....** Values can be set to indent from Left, Right, Top and/or Bottom.

Resizing

- You can resize frame or shape text (change its point size) automatically when resizing frame and shapes. First make sure the **Scale text with object** box is checked in the Text flow dialog (right-click **Text>Text Flow...**) then drag a corner of the selected text object.

Fitting text to a path

Use the Curve Text Wizard or text context toolbar's Curve Text flyout to make artistic text conform to a curved baseline such as a circle, spiral, arc, or a drawn curve.

To flow text along a curve:

Either:

1. If you want to use an existing text object, select the object first. Otherwise, you can enter text in the wizard.

2. Go to **Tools>Curve Text Wizard**.

3. After the first screen, enter text to be placed on the curve. This is not shown if text has already been selected on the page.

4. In the second screen, if an object or outline has already been selected the **Use Current Selection** option will be checked. Uncheck if you want your text to flow along one of the available preset curves then pick a curve on which the text will be placed.

5. Click **Finish** to close the wizard. If using an existing text object, the text will be placed on the curve, line or shape. For text entered via the wizard, you'll have to click to add text of a default size to the page (or drag out the text on the page for a custom size).

- or -

1. Select your artistic text.

2. From the context toolbar, click the down arrow on the Preset Text Paths: button and select a preset curve from the drop-down menu on which the text will flow.

★ You can edit the baseline curve with the Node Tool.

Adding dimension lines and labels

DrawPlus lets you add **dimension lines** with text **labels** showing the distance between two fixed points in a drawing, or the angle formed by three points. For example, you can draw a dimension line along one side of a box, measuring the distance between the two corner points. If you resize the box, the line automatically follows suit, and its label text updates to reflect the new measurement.

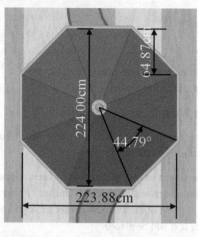

You'll find dimension lines indispensable for planning garden designs (e.g., a garden gazebo plan above), technical diagrams, floor plans, or any drawing where exact measurements and scale are important.

Although they can be drawn anywhere on the page, dimension lines are at their most accurate when attached to **connection points** on objects (see p. 77). When you choose one of the Dimension tools, connection points on page objects become visible on hover over, i.e. when you move the mouse pointer directly over a connection point, a small box appears around it when a connection can be made. For more information on connection points, see Working with connectors on p. 75.

To draw a dimension:

1. Select the **Dimension Tool** from the **Drawing** toolbar's Line flyout. (The flyout shows the icon of the most recently selected tool.)

2. Either, for a **linear dimension** (vertical, horizontal, or slanted), click the respective tool from the Dimension context toolbar:

   - ▮ Vertical Dimension Tool

   - ↔ Horizontal Dimension Tool

   - ↗ Slanted Dimension Tool

Click where you want to start the dimension line (e.g., on a connection point), then drag and release the mouse button where you want to end the line (maybe on another connection point). The illustrations below show the result of dragging between connection points A and B.

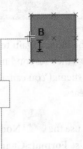

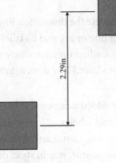

A pair of parallel **extension lines** appears from the two points. Between the two extension lines, the dimension line and its label "float." Click the blue line box to position the floating line and label; drag the red circle within.

Release when the line and label are where you want them. (You can always change the positions later.) Click away to reveal the dimension line.

- or -

For an **angular dimension**, click the **Angular Dimension tool** then click on a point along one side of the desired angle, then drag and release the mouse button at a point along the other side of the angle (points A and B in the illustration below). Click again at the vertex of the angle (point C below). These three points define the starting and ending sides of the angle. Between the two sides, the angle's arc and its label "float," awaiting final positioning. Click again to position the floating elements.

★ Angles are measured anti-clockwise from the starting to the ending side, so choose your three nodes accordingly.

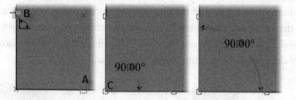

To complete the dimension line, move the mouse again to position the floating line or arc and its label—note that they respond independently—and click when they are where you want them. (You can always change the positions later.) The dimension line appears.

Once you've added a dimension line, you can use the **Node Tool** to freely adjust node and label positions if necessary. Use **Format>Character** to change the font, font size, colour and style of the label text. You can also format the line, including line colour, width, style, or adjust the level of precision with the Dimensions context toolbar.

Spell-checking

The **Spell Checker** lets you check the spelling of selected artistic, frame, or shape text, as well as all text sequentially throughout your DrawPlus document.

Multilingual spell checking is supported by use of over 10 spelling dictionaries. By default, the spelling dictionary is set on program install (according to Windows Control Panel's Regional and Language Options), i.e. your dictionary is set to the operating system's language.

between the pair. The clock struck midnight.. the man was gone, forver into the mist-clad night.

Any detected spelling mistakes or any word not present in the language's dictionary will appear underlined with a red zigzag line.

Alternatively, the **Spell Checker** can be launched to run through your document, spell checking as it goes.

To enhance the power of spell checking, you can add words to the current dictionary that spell checking doesn't yet know about. These could include uncommon words, technical words, or even acronyms and abbreviations.

To check spelling:

1. (Optional) To check specific text, select the artistic, frame or shape text in advance.

2. Choose **Check Spelling...** from the **Tools** menu.

3. (Optional) In the dialog, click **Options...** to set preferences for ignoring words in certain categories, such as words containing numbers or upper/mixed case characters.

4. Enable **Check currently selected objects only** or **Check all text** radio buttons depending on if you want to spell check text selected previously or all text.

5. Click **Start** to begin the spelling check.

When a problem is found, DrawPlus highlights the problem word on the page. The dialog offers alternative suggestions, and you can choose to **Change** or **Ignore** this instance (or all instances with **Change All** or **Ignore All**) of the problem word, with the option of using **Add** to add the problem word to your dictionary. DrawPlus will also let you **Suggest** an alternative.

6. Spell checking continues until you click the **Close** button or the spell-check is completed.

To change to a different spelling language:

1. Go to **Options...** from the **Tools** menu, and select **Spell Checker**.

2. Choose a different **Language** from the drop-down menu, and click **OK**.

> Spell checking can be turned off by selecting "None" as a language type—this could be useful when working with text containing an unmanageable number of unusual terms (perhaps scientific or proprietary terminology).

To check the spelling of a single word:

1. With **Underline mistakes as you type** checked and a language selected (in **Tools>Options>Spell Checker**), select in a marked word, then right-click. You'll see alternative spellings on the context menu.

2. To replace the word, choose an alternative spelling from the menu.

3. To tell DrawPlus to ignore (leave unmarked) all instances of the marked word in the document, choose **Ignore All**.

4. To add the marked word (as spelled) to your personal dictionary, choose **Add to Dictionary**. This means DrawPlus will ignore the word in any drawing.

You can also run the Spell Checker from the context menu by choosing **Check Spelling...**.

> You can make your own custom dictionary via
> Tools>Options>Spelling Dictionary.

Working with Objects

7

Copying, pasting, cutting, and deleting objects

To copy one or more objects to the Windows Clipboard:

1. Select the object(s).

2. Click the **Copy** button on the **Standard** toolbar.

If you're using another Windows application, you can usually copy and paste objects via the Clipboard.

To paste an object from the Clipboard:

- Click the **Paste** button on the **Standard** toolbar.

The standard Paste command inserts a clipboard object onto the page.

> ★ To select the type of object to be pasted from the Clipboard, choose **Paste Special...** from the **Edit** menu.

To cut one or more objects to the Clipboard:

1. Select the object(s).

2. Click the **Cut** button on the **Standard** toolbar.

The object is deleted from the page and a copy is placed on the Windows Clipboard.

To delete one or more objects:

- Select the object(s) with the Pointer, Rotate or Node Tool and press the **Delete** key.

Cloning an object

DrawPlus lets you "clone" or duplicate objects easily using drag-and-drop, and duplicate multiple copies of any object. For duplication, a copy is displayed at the new location and the original object is still kept at the same position—your new copy also possesses the formatting of the original copied object.

Making duplicates

- Select the object while holding down the **Ctrl** key, then drag the copied object to a new position.

> ★ Use duplication when rotating or shearing an object—the result is a new copy at a new angle, possibly overlapping the original object.

Making multiple copies in a grid

If you need to clone single or multiple objects, you can use the **Replicate** feature to avoid repetitive copy and paste operations. For example, you can specify three columns and three rows, for nine identical copies (opposite).

To replicate an object:

1. Select an object. Remember to size the object to be cloned and place it in a convenient starting position—usually the top-left of the page.

2. Choose **Replicate...** from the **Tools** menu.

3. In the dialog, set the Grid size by choosing number of columns or rows. Objects are cloned into this grid arrangement (but can be moved subsequently into any position).

4. Set an X and Y spacing (horizontal and vertical gap) between objects if necessary. The feature comes in handy for creating repetitive patterns or producing artwork for label sheets.

5. Click **OK**.

> ★ For replicating multiple objects on different layers, enable the **Edit All Layers** button on the Layers tab. Now, instead of working with the layers one at a time, we can include all objects (once selected) on all layers, permitting perfect replication.

Applying a transform

The Transform feature lets you make multiple copies of one or more selected objects, with a transformation applied to each successive copy in the series.

For example, a butterfly can be made to fly with a transform of 15° rotation, 113% scaling, 4 copies, and an X offset of 2.2cm.

To create a transform:

1. Select an object then choose **Transform...** from the **Tools** menu.

2. From the dialog, specify the type of transformation (rotation and/or scaling), the number of copies, and a positional offset between copies.

> ★ Transforms are a quick way to generate elements for a stopframe animation sequence involving rotation or directional changes.

Making "in-between" copies of two objects

Blending is yet another useful way of making multiple copies by in-betweening two different objects for a "morphing" effect. For details, see Creating blends on p. 188.

Cropping an object

DrawPlus includes the **Crop Tool** for cropping objects (and images) on the page. Cropping discards unwanted "outer" regions of an object while keeping the remainder

visible.

To crop an object:

1. Select an object and then on the **Drawing** toolbar, click the ⬚ **Crop Tool**.

2. Click and drag an edge or corner handle towards the centre of the object.

Applying the **Rule of Thirds** grid helps the composition of your design during cropping.

To apply the Rule of Thirds:

1. Select your object and click the **Crop Tool**.

2. On the Crop context toolbar, click ⊞ Show/Hide Thirds Grid.

3. A 3 x 3 grid is superimposed on top of the object.

4. Drag a corner or edge grid handle to crop the image. As you do so, the grid repositions itself.

5. Manipulate the image to improve its framing.

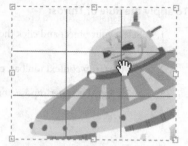

- Click and drag on the cropped photo to pan the image. For best results, aim to position your main subject of interest at a point where any two gridlines intersect.

- To rotate or zoom into or out of the object, use the adjacent control bar.

- Alternatively use equivalent button pairings on the context toolbar.

🔍➕ 🔍➖ **Zoom In/Out**

↻ ↺ **Rotate anti-clockwise/clockwise**

- To select the crop window.

  Select Crop ⊓ from the control bar.

- To select cropped objects.

  Click Select Cropped Object(s) 🖼 from the control bar. The original uncropped object is selected.

- Uncrop a cropped area.

  Click 🗙 Uncrop with the crop window selected.

- Crop an object using a preset shape.

  With the crop window selected, choose a QuickShape from the  □ Crop Shape ▼ drop-down menu.

- To reshape a cropped area.

With the crop window selected...

- Choose  **Convert to Curves** on the **Arrange** tab.

- Select the Node Tool, then drag the object's **nodes**. For details, see Editing lines and shapes.

Copying an object's formatting

Format Painter is used to copy one object's line and fill properties directly to another object, including between line/shape and text objects.

To apply one object's formatting to another:

1. Select the object whose formatting you wish to copy.

2. Click Format Painter on the **Standard** toolbar. When you click the button, the selected object's formatting is "picked up."

3. Click another object to apply the first object's formatting to it. The second object becomes selected.

4. To select another object without pasting the formatting, click it with the **Shift** key down.

5. To cancel Format Painter mode, press **Esc**, click on a blank area, or choose any tool button.

For copy formatting from one text object to another, a number of other text properties (font, style, and so on) besides line and fill are passed along at the same time.

Moving objects

You can move any selected object anywhere you want and drop it back onto the page or pasteboard by releasing the mouse button.

To move one or more objects:

1. Select the object(s).

2. Click and drag the 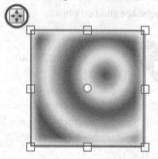 **Move** button. The object moves.

- or -

Click within the selection and drag.

★ Note that the Pointer cursor changed to become a 🖳 Move cursor.

💡 Use the keyboard arrows to move in increments.

💡 To set exact horizontal and vertical positions, use the Transform tab.

Cutting up objects

It is possible to cut any object (or image for that matter) by using the **Knife Tool** (**Drawing** toolbar). You can cut along a freeform or straight line drawn across your object(s), leaving you with separate fragments of the original.

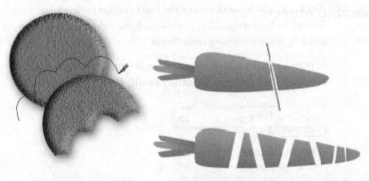

freeform cut
(using Bump profile)

straight line cut

Cutting with a freeform or straight line is possible by drawing the line across the object (or by sweeping the knife cut in and out of the object multiple times in a zig-zag pattern). By hovering over resulting "split" fragments you can click an unwanted fragment to delete. Alternatively, you can deselect the Knife Tool to move the cut fragments apart (see carrot above).

Up to now you may have only performed straight cuts, but you can use the Knife Tool's context toolbar to cut with more sophisticated "shaped" **cutting profiles** (e.g., Wavy, Shark Fin, Bump, plus many more) or preset knife paths (cookie cutters) based on QuickShapes. The context toolbar is also used to modify any applied cutting profile.

To cut selected objects (freeform or straight line):

> Ensure Edit All Layers button on the Layers tab is enabled if you
> want to cut through selected objects on multiple layers.

1. Select the ✐ **Knife Tool** on the **Drawing** toolbar's 🖌 ▾ **Vector Edit** flyout.

2. (Optional) Use **Smoothness** on the tool's context toolbar to set how regular the freeform cutting line is—click the right arrow and drag the slider right for increasing smoothness.

3. (Optional) By default, you'll get a straight cutting profile, but for regular-shaped cuts, pick a **Cutting Profile** from the context toolbar.

∿∿∿ Pinking	▾
───── Straight	▴
⎍⎍⎍ Square	
∿∿∿ Wavy	
∿∿∿ Pinking	
⋀⋀⋀ Double ZigZag	
⋀⋀⋀ Triple ZigZag	
⌐⌐⌐ Diagonal	
⋁⋁⋁ Saw	
⋏⋏⋏ Spike	
⌐⌐⌐ Fence	
⌐⌐⌐ Spacer	

If required, adjust the **Wavelength** and/or **Amplitude** for your shaped cut.

4. Using the cursor, drag a **freeform** line across any object(s) you would like to split (unselected objects on which the line traverses will not be split). Instead, press the **Ctrl** key as you drag for a **straight** line.

5. Hover over, then click to remove the unwanted cut area(s).

- or -

With the Pointer Tool, drag the newly split fragments apart instead.

Instead of performing a freeform (or straight) cut, you can cut using preset cutter shapes. The cutting shape can be resized or "morphed" to fit your object design, just as for QuickShapes (see p. 68).

To cut out selected objects using cookie cutters:

1. From the Knife Tool's context toolbar, click to expand the **Preset Knife Path** flyout.

2. Click a preset shape to apply it to your object as a cutout.

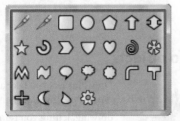

The first and second options offer an easy way to jump between freehand and straight line cutting.

3. The shape is applied to the object. Adjust the size and shape using the surrounding square handles and round nodes, respectively.

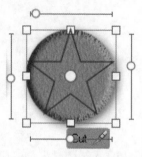

4. Click the **Cut** button in the lower-right corner, then click the unwanted area under the cursor to create your new cutout shape.

Erasing and adding to objects

DrawPlus lets you take a "virtual" eraser to your drawing, letting you remove portions of your selected object(s) on an individual layer or across multiple layers. The extent of erasing can be controlled depending on the tool's currently set erasing nib width and pressure setting (if using a graphics tablet).

The flipside of erasing is "**adding to**" (i.e., augmenting), a technique to add or "grow" a vector objects' boundaries—great for reshaping an existing object or to grow a vector shape from scratch. This may be especially useful when creating an unusual filled shape.

To erase portions of a selected object:

1. Select the ✏ **Erase Tool** on the **Drawing** toolbar's 🖌▾ Vector Edit flyout.

2. (Optional) From the context toolbar, choose a **Nib** style (circle, square, or diamond) and/or set a **Width** to define the erase width that will be cut.

3. Position the 🖑 cursor, and drag over an object's edge. You'll see the area to be erased area being drawn temporarily (use the **Ctrl** key to redefine the erase area while drawing).

4. Release the mouse button to erase the area drawn.

To add to a selected object:

1. Select the 🖌 **Freeform Paint Tool** on the **Drawing** toolbar's 🖌▾ Vector Edit flyout.

2. (Optional) From the context toolbar, set a **Width** to define the nib width which will be drawn.

3. (Optional) Disable **Select-on-Create** if you want to create new objects every time you use the tool (you might want to create a series of shapes without switching tools).

4. Position the 🖑 cursor over the object and drag over an object boundary. You'll see blue shading which represents the area to be

added. (You can use the **Ctrl** key to redefine the painted area while holding down the mouse button).

5.   Release the mouse button to reshape the object to include the newly drawn area.

★   If you add to or erase from a bitmap, QuickShape, or artistic text, they will be converted to curves, preventing further editing in their original form.

★   For Stopframe animation, consider using either tool as a quick way to modify object shapes frame-by-frame.

Resizing objects

It's fairly likely that you may want to resize an object to fit into your current design. DrawPlus offers a range of resizing options directly on the object, as well as more precise resizing via keyboard arrows or the Transform tab.

To resize an object to a fixed aspect ratio:

1.   Select the object(s) with the ![pointer] **Pointer Tool**.

2.   Position the cursor over one of the object's handles—you will notice that the cursor changes to a double-headed Size cursor.

3.   Drag from a corner handle (above) to resize in two dimensions (by moving two edges), while maintaining the selection's aspect ratio (proportions).

★   To resize about the object centre instead, press the **Ctrl** key as you drag.

To allow free resizing of an object to any aspect ratio:

With the **Shift** key depressed, drag from an object's corner handle. This resizes in two directions.

If you drag an object's side handles, you'll stretch or squash the object in one direction.

> 💡 You can also make fine resizing adjustments via the keyboard or from the Transform tab.

Rotating and shearing objects

The **Rotate Tool** lets you both rotate and shear (slant) one or more objects.

To rotate one or more objects around a centre point:

1. Click 🔄 **Rotate Tool** on the **Drawing** toolbar's Selection Tool flyout.

2. Click to select the object, then hover over a corner handle and, when you see the cursor change, drag in the direction in which you want to rotate the object then release the mouse. (Use **Shift** key for rotating in 15 degree intervals.)

You'll notice the angle of rotation displayed around the object's centre of rotation ◐. Note that when rotating objects, dimensions will be temporarily displayed during the operation.

To change the centre point of rotation:

1. Move the centre of rotation ◐ away from its original position to any position on the page. The marker can also be moved to be outside the object—ideal for rotating grouped objects around a central point.

2. Drag the rotate pointer to a new rotation angle—the object will rotate about the new pivot.

Besides being able to rotate an object, the Rotate Tool allows you to skew or "shear" it.

To shear or copy shear an object:

1. Select **Rotate Tool** on the **Drawing** toolbar's Selection flyout.

2. Click to select the object(s), hover over any side handle (not a corner handle) until you see the Shear cursor.

3. Hold the mouse down and drag the pointer in the direction in which you want to shear the object, then release.

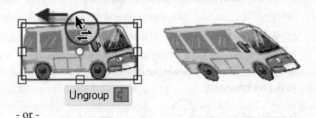

- or -

- Select the object, go to the Transform tab and enter a **Shear** value.

To copy shear, use the **Ctrl** key while dragging—this preserves the original object, while shearing the new copied object as you drag.

To undo the rotation or shear (restore the original object):

- Double-click the object.

DrawPlus also provides the following methods for controlling rotation. (These don't apply to shear.)

Flipping objects

You can flip objects horizontally (left to right; top and bottom stay the same) or vertically (top to bottom; left and right stay the same).

To flip an object:

- Select the object(s) with one of the selection tools (Pointer, Rotate, or Node).

- To flip the selection left to right, click **Flip Horizontal** on the Arrange tab. (Top and bottom stay the same.)

- To flip the selection top to bottom, click **Flip Vertical** on the Arrange tab. (Left and right stay the same.)

Finding objects

When you create any object in your DrawPlus drawing you're actually creating an object name for that drawing. This serves several purposes: to uniquely identify objects when using the Layers tab and to allow objects to be targeted by ActionScript (in Keyframe animation).

Object names are visible in the Layers tab—they are created on a selected layer automatically as you draw the object. Many objects are given the same names such as "Bitmap", "Quick Ellipse", "Curve, 2 Nodes"; you may like to rename each object to make them distinct from each other (making them clearly identifiable).

You can also name groups within DrawPlus using the same principle; consider a garden project where you could name specific objects in your garden.

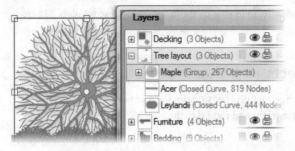

DrawPlus lets you search for your named objects (or groups) to allow resizing, rotating, transforming, or any other operation by using the **Find Objects** dialog; it can locate the object or group on the current layer, page or the entire document (shown).

Find What:

Maple

Look In:

Whole Document

☐ Match Whole Word
☐ Match Case
☐ Search Up

> ★ Objects or groups that have not been named manually will never be included in the search.
>
> ★ To change an object's or group's name, see Managing objects on layers.

To find an object or group:

1. Select **Find Object...** from the **Edit** menu.

2. From the dialog, enter the individual object or group name you want to search for in the **Find What** box. As partial matching is supported by default you can also search for the beginning of objects' names, i.e. searching for "frog" would locate objects named "frog1", "frog2", "frogs legs", etc.

3. In the **Look In** drop-down menu, restrict the search to the Current Layer or Current Page. Alternatively, search throughout the Whole Document.

4. (Optional) Limit your search to **Match Whole Word** or **Match Case** by enabling the check boxes. To search from the bottom of your layers upward, check the **Search Up** check box.

5. Click the **Find Next** button to perform your search. The first matching object is shown selected and zoomed to selection (ready for editing!).

6. (Optional) For more than one object located, click the **Find Next** button again to jump to the next matching object.

Locking/unlocking an object

So you may have moved or resized a few objects and don't want to risk moving, resizing or deleting them. The solution is to lock them to prevent accidental changes from occurring.

To lock/unlock an object:

1. Select the single or grouped object.

2. Choose **Lock Position** or **Unlock Position** from the **Arrange** menu. When you lock the object, the cursor changes to a lock symbol.

> You can still alter a locked object's fill, line, or transparency properties.

Grouping objects

The advantage of converting a set of objects into a group is that it is easier to select and edit the objects all at the same time. The only requirement for grouping is that multiple objects are selected in advance (see p. 125).

To create a group from a multiple selection:

- Click Group below the selection.

To ungroup (turn a group back into a multiple selection):

- Click Ungroup below the selection.

To ungroup multiple groups within a group:

- Select **Ungroup All** from the **Arrange** menu.

Once grouped, simply clicking on any member of a group selects the group object. In general, any operation you carry out on the group affects each member of the group. Property changes applied to a group—such as changing line or fill—will alter all the objects that make up the group.

> Objects within groups can be selected with the Ctrl key and edited without having to ungroup your grouped objects.

Combining, cropping, and joining objects

DrawPlus includes some powerful tools to carve new shapes out of old shapes— the **Combine**, **Crop**, **Clip**, **Add**, **Subtract**, and **Intersect** buttons on the **Arrange tab**. Combine, Crop and Clip work a bit differently from Add, Subtract and Intersect (considered as "Join" commands). It's worth keeping the distinctions in mind:

- With Combine, Crop and Clip, you're creating a temporary composite object where two or more component objects used to overlap. This combination, like a group, can be broken apart later with **Crop>Uncrop** on the **Arrange** menu.

- With the Join commands, you actually produce a permanent new object out of any selected objects. The action can't be reversed, except by using the **Undo** command. A Joined object can be edited with the Node Tool, while a combined, cropped or clipped object cannot.

Combine

Merges two or more objects into a composite object, with a clear "hole" where their filled regions overlap. The composite takes the line and fill of the bottom object. Click button again to **Break Apart**.

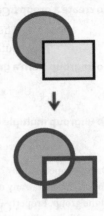

Crop and Clip flyout

Provides four cropping or clipping functions as follows:

• **Crop to Top Object**
The bottom object is cropped to the outline of the top object.

• **Crop to Bottom Object**
The top object is cropped to the outline of the bottom object.

• **Clip to Top Object**
The bottom object is clipped to the outline of the top object.

• **Clip to Bottom Object**
The top object is clipped to the outline of the bottom object.

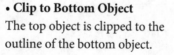

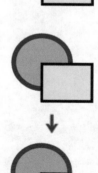

Join/Add Creates one new object that's the sum of any two selected objects, whether or not they overlap.

The objects need not be overlapping.

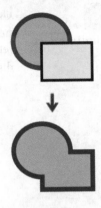

Join/Subtract Discards the overlap between the top and bottom object. The top object is also discarded.

Useful as a quick way of truncating shapes and pictures with another object.

Be sure the objects are overlapping!

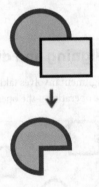

Join/Intersect

like Subtract, requires overlapping objects—it retains the overlap and discards the rest.

Aligning and distributing objects

Alignment involves taking a group of selected objects and aligning them all in one operation—the operation is applied to all of the objects selected.

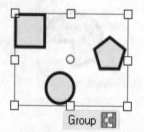

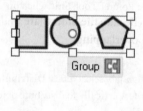

You can also distribute objects, so that your objects (as a multiple selection) are spread evenly between the endmost objects on your page. Alternatively, check the **Spaced** option and corresponding measurement value to set a specific distance between each object.

To align two or more objects:

1. Using the Pointer Tool, **Shift**-click on all the objects you want to align, or draw a marquee box around them (or use **Edit>Select All**), to create a multiple selection.

2. From context toolbar, Align tab, or **Arrange>Align Objects**, select an option for vertical alignment (Align Top, Centre Vertically, or Align Bottom) or horizontal alignment (Align Left, Centre Horizontally, Align Right) of an object. Object means the last selected object for **Shift**-click multiple selection or the farthest back in Z-order for marquee multiple selection.

To align one or more objects with a page edge:

*   Follow the steps above, but check the **Include Page** option.

If selected, the page is added to the set of objects included in the alignment, e.g. selecting **Align Top** aligns all of the objects in the selection to the top of the page. If only one object is selected, page-edge alignment is automatic.

To distribute two or more objects:

1. Using the Pointer Tool, **Shift**-click on all the objects you want to distribute, or draw a marquee box around them, to create a multiple selection.

2. In the Align tab, select **Distribute Horizontally** or **Distribute Vertically** to distribute objects vertically or horizontally, respectively.

3. Check the **Spaced** option to set a fixed distance between vertically or horizontally distributed objects (otherwise the objects distribute evenly between endmost items).

Ordering objects

Think of the objects on a page as being stacked or piled on top of each other. The front-most object is the one on top of the stack. Each time you create a new object, it goes in front of the objects already there. But you can move any object to any **level** in the ordering sequence, and obtain sophisticated drawing effects by learning how to manipulate the front/back relationship of objects.

As an example, we've used a camera lens to illustrate ordering.

Notice how the lens possesses a "realistic" look by blending overlapped composite objects.

Gradient and solid fills combine to simulate three-dimensional objects (with reflections, highlights and shading).

> ★ Don't confuse the concept of object ordering with that of layers in the document. Layers are created by the artist to logically separate sections of a design for better drawing management.

To change the object's order (from the Arrange tab):

- To shift the selected object's position to the front of other objects (on top), choose the **Bring to Front** button.

- To shift the object's position one step toward the front, choose **Forward One**.

- To shift the object's position one step toward the back, choose **Back One**.

- To shift the selected object's position behind other objects (on the bottom), choose **Send to Back**.

Working with layers

If you are drawing something simple, you don't really need to make use of layers—you can do all your work on the single layer that every new document has. However, if you're creating something a little more tricky then layers can be a vital aid in separating objects into independent sets. You can think of layers as transparent sheets of paper upon which you can draw your objects.

Layers are useful when you're working on a complex design where it makes sense to separate one cluster of objects from another. The whole drawing is produced by piling up the layers and viewing all of the objects on all of the layers; you can choose which layer you are editing and thus make changes without fear of modifying anything on another layer. In essence, by building up your drawing from multiple layers you make it much easier to edit.

Each layer is situated along with other layers (if present) within a stack on the **Layers tab**—the uppermost layer is applied over any lower layer on the page. You can also expand each layer entry for a tree view of objects associated with that layer (see the "Sky" layer opposite). Each object entry can be clicked to select the object in your workspace, and you can name your objects at any time.

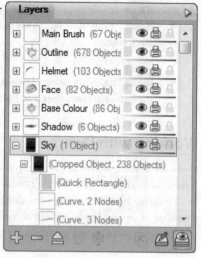

The tab allows layers to be created, renamed, deleted, reordered, frozen, and merged.

Thumbnail previews of each layer or object show before each entry—hover your cursor over the thumbnail for a larger preview.

In order to create a new object on a particular layer, you'll first need to "activate" (select) that layer.

To select a particular layer:

• Click a layer name in the Layers tab.

To add a new layer:

• In the Layers tab, click the [+] **Add Layer** button to add a new layer above the currently selected layer.

To rename a layer:

• To rename a layer to something more meaningful, click on the selected layer's name and type to add your new name (you can also make an insertion point to edit the existing text). A good example would be to rename the initial Layer 1 to be called "Sky" (as above).

To delete a layer:

- In the Layers tab, select the layer's name and click the [icon] **Delete Layer** button.

★ If you delete a layer, all of the objects on it are lost! So if you want to keep any of them, move them to another layer first.

You can move layers up or down in the stacking order to place their objects in front or behind those on other layers, move objects to specific layers, and even merge layers.

To move a layer in the stacking order:

- [icons] In the Layers tab, select the layer's entry, then click the **Move Layer Up** or **Move Layer Down** button to move the layer up or down in the list, respectively.

  - or -

- Drag the selected layer to a new position in the layer stack.

Remember that objects on layers are drawn in the order in which the layers were initially added to the Layers tab. Put another way: the bottom layer in the Layers tab stack is drawn first then the second bottom, third bottom etc. A background layer should be the bottom layer in the Layers tab stack.

The standard object ordering commands (Forward One, Back One, etc.) can be used on a layer, affecting an object's level within the layer it currently occupies. For more information, see Ordering objects on p. 132.

At some point you may be confident that objects on separate layers can be managed on the same layer without compromising layer control. Merging layers enables this and will help to keep your layer management simpler. This rationalization is possible via the **Merge** button.

To merge a layer:

1. Activate the layer you want to merge **to** by clicking its entry. The layer is highlighted in blue. (Note that the active layer becomes uppermost in the workspace.)

2. With the **Ctrl** key pressed, select a single or multiple layers that you want to merge into the activated layer (the layers are framed with a blue border).

3. Click the ⬍ **Merge** button. The contents of the merged layer(s) appear on the active layer and the previously selected layers disappear.

If you're working on an especially complex document you can temporarily freeze a layer (and its objects) via right -click finished with to speed up performance. The layer is rasterized to a user-defined DPI (96 DPI by default) and is not editable until it is unfrozen (although it remains visible).

Layer Properties

Layer properties allow you to assign paper textures, make layers invisible, non-printable and/or locked. An object's selection handle colour can also be defined based on its current layer. You can perform these operations directly from the Layers tab (or by double-clicking or right-click on a layer entry):

- Click the ▢ **Paper textures** icon to apply a texture to object(s) on a layer. The displayed dialog, offers a Paper Textures category from which you can choose a texture from a selection of texture thumbnails.

- Click/unclick the 👁 **Visible** icon to show/hide the layer and any objects on it.

- Click/unclick the 🖶 **Printable** icon to include/exclude the layer in PDF output or hardcopy printouts. Non-printing layers are handy "for information only."
  Note: Hidden layers will still print, as long as they are checked as printable.

- Click/unclick the 🔓 **Locked** column to allow/prevent objects on the
  layer from being moved, deleted, or resized. (Clicking 🔓 on the
  Layer's entry locks the layer, which will then shown as 🔒).

- To set a Selection colour, double-click the layer's name. From the
  dialog, click the colour swatch (e.g., ■) and choose a colour from the
  dialog. Assigning different colours to layers means that you can
  quickly verify that a pasted object has gone to the correct layer, i.e. the
  box surrounding the object on a layer always adopts the Selection
  colour assigned to the layer. The layer shows its current selection
  colour as a thin colour strip under the layer property icons.

Managing objects on layers

A useful feature of the Layers tab is that you can see objects or even groups of
objects, under the layer on which they were created. This gives you the option of
selecting an object or group from the tab as opposed to from the page itself.
Either group or object can be named, and once named, located on your page.

To add objects to a particular layer:

- When drawn, objects are added to the selected layer automatically.
  This is why it is a good idea to check which layer you are currently
  working on!

To select objects on a particular layer:

- In the Layers tab, if the ✏️ **Edit All Layers** button is disabled, click
  the chosen layer and either:

  - Click the layer's object on the page.
    - or -

  - In the Layers tab, click the ⊞ Expand icon on the chosen layer
    entry to reveal all associated objects. You'll see objects named
    automatically, e.g. "Curve, 2 Nodes", "Closed Curve, 5 Nodes",
    "Quick Rectangle", etc., each with their own preview. The front-
    most object in your drawing always appears at the top of the
    layer's listed objects (the order reflects the Z-order).

⊟ ━ **Shadow** (6 Objects)
   ━ (Curve, 4 Nodes)
   ━ (Curve, 3 Nodes)
   ━ (Curve, 4 Nodes)
   ━ (Curve, 2 Nodes)
   ━ (Curve, 7 Nodes)
   ━ (Curve, 2 Nodes)

This tree view greatly improves the ability to select and manage nested objects in more complex drawings. It's also great for visualizing your object order.

To help you locate objects more easily in the future, they can be renamed (click and type on the name) to something more meaningful, and can be further identified by their thumbnail previews. Objects can also be searched for via **Find Objects...** on the **Edit** menu.

The object on the page is selected when selection handles appear on the object and the displayed bounding box reflects the selected layer's colour.

To select any object on any layer:

Initially, objects which are on layers that are not selected are also visible, but you may find that you can't select an object as it is on a different layer. This can be slightly confusing at first as you frantically click on an object to no effect! But of course, you can change this state of affairs.

- If 🖼 **View All Layers** is enabled (the default), all layers set as visible appear in the edit window, regardless of which layer you're currently working on. Disabling this button lets you see only objects on the current layer, as long as it's visible. (If both **Visible** and **View All Layers** are unchecked, you won't see anything!)

- If ✏ **Edit All Layers** (available only if **View All Layers** is enabled) is disabled (the default), you can only select objects in the current layer.

Enabling this button lets you select any object on any visible layer. You can press the Tab key repeatedly to cycle between objects in order.

- If ![icon] **Auto-Select Layer** is enabled (available only if **Edit All Layers** is enabled), you'll automatically select an object's layer and the object entry in the Layers tab as you select it on the page. This stops you from having to jump back to the Layers tab to set the layer to be active after object selection.

To change an object's or group's name:

1. In the Layers tab, expand the layer entry to which an object or group belongs.

2. Select the object/group, then click on its name.

3. At the insertion point, type a new name then either press **Enter** or click away from the tab.

To move an object to another layer:

- Select the object, right-click and choose **Move Object to Layer...**. From the dialog, select the specific destination layer.
  - or -

- Select the object, right-click and choose **Move Object to Active Layer**. The object moves to whichever layer was previously active.

To freeze any object on any layer:

- Select an object (or multiple objects with the **Ctrl** key), right-click and select **Freeze**. To unfreeze, click the ❄ snowflake displayed at the end of its object entry.

> ✦ Like frozen layers, frozen objects are not editable.

Fill, Lines, Colours, and Transparency

8

Setting fill properties

Any closed shape, such as a closed curve or QuickShape, or text has an interior region that can be filled. The fill type can be solid, gradient, bitmap or plasma. Those that use a single colour are solid fills. Let's take a moment to run through them.

Fill types fall into several basic categories, illustrated above:

- **Solid fills**, as their name implies, use a single colour.

- **Gradient fills** provide a gradation or spectrum of colours between two or more "key" colours. Mesh fills work like gradient fills but with a more complex fill path.

- **Bitmap** and **Plasma fills** apply bitmapped images or patterns to the object, each with unique properties. Think of bitmap fills as named "pictures" that fill shapes. Plasma (or "fractal") fills use randomized patterns, useful for simulating cloud or shadow effects.

Solid colours

Applying a fill is easy, whether you're selecting a custom colour from the **Colour tab** or a preset colour from a whole range of colour swatches in the **Swatch tab**.

The Colour tab can operate in several modes available from a drop-down menu—HSL Colour Wheel (shown), HSL Colour Box, HSL Sliders, RGB Sliders, CMYK Sliders and Tinting. We'll concentrate on the HSL Colour Wheel which is very popular amongst drawing professionals.

The HSL Colour Wheel is made up of four key components—the line/fill swatches, the outer Hue wheel, Saturation/Lightness triangle, and an Opacity slider.

The Line/Fill swatches govern whether the selected colour is applied as a line colour, solid fill, or both simultaneously.

The small circles shown in the wheel and triangle indicate the current setting for hue and saturation/lightness, respectively. Drag either circle around to adjust the overall HSL value.

A **Tinting** option in the Colour tab's drop-down menu (not shown above) allows a percentage of shade/tint to be applied to your colour.

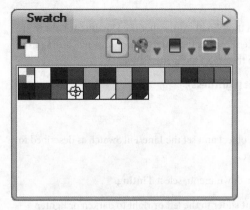

By comparison, the Swatch tab hosts a vast array of colour swatches for solid, gradient, plasma, and bitmap fills.

You may notice a registration colour swatch in the palette. You can use this for professional colour separation printing.

To apply a solid fill colour via the Colour tab:

1. Select the object(s) and display the Studio's **Colour tab**.

2. Set the Line/Fill Swatch at the top-left of the tab so the Fill Swatch appears in front of the Line swatch. This defines where the colour will be applied. Alternatively, apply colour to both line and fill simultaneously by clicking **Link** on the swatch.

3. Choose a colour display mode (HSL Colour Wheel, HSL Colour Box, HSL Sliders, RGB Sliders, or CMYK Sliders) from the drop-down menu.

4. Select a colour from the display.

Exact colour values can be set in a **Colour Selector** dialog available by either double-clicking the swatch or from **Format>Fill...**.

To apply a solid fill colour via the Swatch tab:

1. Select the object(s) and display the Studio's **Swatch tab**.

2. Set the Line/Fill Swatch at the top-left of the tab so the Fill Swatch appears in front of the Line Swatch.

3. Pick a thumbnail from either the **Document Palette** or from another palette shown in the **Palettes** drop-down list (drag from the thumbnail onto the object as an alternative).

To change a fill's shade/tint (lightness):

1. Select the object and set the Line/Fill Swatch as described for the Colour tab above.

2. From the tab's drop-down menu, select **Tinting**.

3. Drag the **Shade/Tint** slider to the left or right to darken or lighten your starting colour, respectively (the original colour is set at 0%). You can also enter a percentage value in the box (entering 0 or dragging the pointer back to its original position reverts to the original colour).

To apply a gradient, bitmap, or plasma fill to one or more objects:

As for applying a solid colour fill with the Swatch tab but:

• Instead of using a solid colour palette, pick a relevant category from the **Gradient** or **Bitmap** galleries, and pick your required thumbnail from the displayed presets (drag from the thumbnail onto the object as an alternative).

For solid, gradient or Plasma fills, you can then edit **colour(s) and shade/tint** (lightness). For gradient and plasma fills, the fill **path** (coverage) can also be edited (see Working with gradient fills on p. 155).

To edit an object's fill colour(s) and tint:

1. Right-click the object and choose **Format>Fill...**.

2. From the Colour Selector dialog's Models tab, optionally choose a different colour model (such as RGB or CMYK) from the **Model** drop-down menu.

3. Use the vertical slider to the immediate right of the colour space window to set your colour value (or use the input box).

4. Click anywhere in the colour space window then drag the marker around to fine-tune your colour selection.

> An **Opacity** level can be applied at the same time that a colour is applied; this leads to powerful colour/opacity combinations on solid fills, or on gradient and plasma fill paths. (See Setting opacity on p. 162.)
>
> For gradient or bitmap transparency effects (see p. 164), use the Transparency Tool or Transparency tab.

To apply no fill:

Set an empty interior for objects by using the:

*   **Colour tab**: Click ☒ **No Fill** in the bottom-left corner of the Line/Fill Swatch (Colour tab), which represents either None (an empty interior for objects with line/fill properties) or Original (for pictures only, to reset the object to its original colours).

    - or -

*   **Swatch tab**: Choose the first swatch, ☒ **None**, from any gallery.

Setting line properties

All lines, including those that enclose shapes, have numerous properties, including colour, style, line ends, weight, join (corner), and cap (end).

Using the Studio's Line tab, you can adjust **plain line** properties for any freeform, straight, or curved line, as well as for the edge of a shape, image or artistic text.

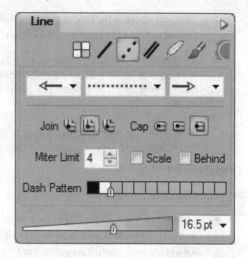

★ To change line colour, see Setting fill properties on p. 143.

★ If needed, any custom line can be saved for future use (see the Line Styles tab). The tab also offers an extensive range of decorative chain lines.

Changing line style

A series of buttons arranged along the top of the Line tab set the line style. **No line**, **Solid**, **Dash**, **Double**, **Calligraphic**, and **Brush Stroke** styles can be applied to freeform lines, and outlines of shapes, images and artistic text alike.

The last **Edge Effect** style applies fringed edges to images and text with specially designed Edge brushes.

To change line style:

- Simply click a button to set the line style—only one style can be set any one time. Pick another button to jump to that style.

Once a style is selected you can choose line ends for most styles (except Brush Stroke and Edge Effect). For some styles, variations are also available. For example, for a Dash or Double line style, additional dash patterns (below) and double line options can be selected.

Custom...

To select a line end:

- From the ⬛ drop-down menus, pick a line start and end.

Other styles such as Dash and Calligraphic offer further customization of the chosen style.

Two styles called [icon] **Brush Stroke** and [icon] **Edge Effect** let you apply a brush, chosen from the Brushes tab, to your line or your object's edge. You'll see your current brush shown in the Line tab. Both effects look great when applied to artistic text titles or to picture edges (see below).

In the above example, a white brush is used around the title text and a stylish "painted" edge has been applied (remember to pick an Edge brush category from the Brushes tab).

Changing line caps and joins

The Line tab also lets you vary a line's **Cap** (end) and the **Join** (corner) where two lines intersect. Both properties tend to be more conspicuous on thicker lines; joins are more apparent with more acute angles. The respective button icons clearly communicate each setting:

Rounded
Line Cap

Extended
Line Cap

Flat
Line Cap

Bevelled
Join

Sharp
Join

Rounded
Join

The ☑ Behind check box controls line width relative to object size—useful with very small objects or when resizing text. When checked, the inner half of the object's line appears behind its fill; otherwise, the whole line appears in front of the line.

Check the ☑ Scale check box to automatically expand and contract the line thickness in proportion to the object size (or uncheck to make the line's thickness remain unchanged). When scaling text, for example, you might either want the border to remain the same width, or change in proportion to the overall characters.

Changing line width

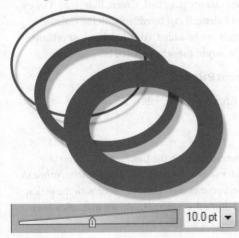

On a selected line, curve, or shape (opposite), drag the **Weight** slider in the Line tab. To turn off the line, set the box to 0.0pt.

10.0 pt ▾

Defining solid line and fill colours

When you're applying a **solid fill** or **line colour** using the Studio's Swatch tab, you choose a colour from one of several colour **palettes**, arranged as a gallery of colour swatch thumbnails. Different palettes can be loaded but only one palette is displayed at any one time. Several of the colour palettes are based on "themed" colours while the remaining palettes are based on industry-standard colour models, i.e.

- **RGB**: Red, Green and Blue (default)

- **CMYK**: Cyan, Magenta, Yellow and Black

Palettes can be loaded, created, deleted and saved as discussed later in Managing colours and palettes on p. 154.

Changing the set of gallery colours

Colours are added manually or automatically from the Colour tab or taken directly from a drawing object's line/fill into the user's **Document Palette**. The palette also stores commonly used colours (e.g., Red, Green, Blue, etc.). Once a colour is stored in the Document Palette, it can be edited with the Colour Selector dialog at any time. Colours can be added, edited, deleted, or renamed within the Document Palette as in any of the other Swatch tab's palettes.

To add a colour to the Document Palette:

- Select a colour mixed from the Colour tab.

   - or -

1. Use the **Colour Selector** on the Colour tab to select any colour on your computer screen. Click on the dropper icon, move to the target area and select your chosen pickup colour with the pickup cursor (if needed, hold down the mouse button for magnification). The colour is picked up in the adjacent swatch.

2. Click this swatch to transfer the colour to the **Fill** swatch.

If the colour doesn't already exist in the Swatch tab's Document Palette, a new thumbnail appears for it.

To add a new gallery colour:

1.   Display the **Document Palette** from the Swatch tab.

2.   Right-click anywhere in the tab and choose **Add...**.

3.   From the Colour Selector dialog, click on a new position in the colour space window to set a new colour. Alternatively, enter values in the adjacent input boxes.

4.   Click **OK**.

> ✎ You can also define a new gallery colour while editing an object's line or fill, as described below. Click the Colour Selector's Options button, then choose Add to Palette.

To redefine an existing gallery colour:

1.   Right-click a sample in any palette (Swatch tab) and choose **Edit...**.

2.   Choose a different colour from the colour spectrum in the Colour Selector dialog.

3.   Click **OK**. The colour and its thumbnail are permanently updated.

To delete a gallery colour:

- Right-click its solid colour thumbnail in any palette (Swatch tab) and choose **Delete**.

If any existing objects use a colour, if you delete it, the objects will retain it, but only as a local (object) fill.

You can also change the definition of any preset colour or fill that appears in the Swatch tab. The process is comparable to adjusting an object's "local" fill, but your change will be permanently available as an updated gallery thumbnail for future use.

Using the Colour Selector

The Colour Selector is a complementary dialog to the Colour and Swatch tabs and is accessible by double-clicking one of the Colour tab's swatch or from **Format>Fill**. It lets you choose a colour to apply from a range of different palettes and allows you to mix custom colours.

- The **Models tab** displays the colour space of several established colour models: RGB (red, green blue), HSL (hue, saturation, lightness), CMYK (cyan, magenta, yellow, black), PANTONE® colors, or registration colour.

- The **Palette tab** displays the colours currently present in the Swatch tab's Document Palette, i.e. your drawing's current palette. The Document Palette can be saved as described in the sub-topic Managing colour and palettes.

Managing colours and palettes

DrawPlus ships with a varied selection of **palettes**, stored separately as .PLT files. The RGB and CMYK palettes can be loaded, along with other "themed" palettes including Earth, Pastels, and Soft Tones. The "themed" palettes offer an alternative to using the RGB and CMYK palettes. Palettes can also be created, deleted and, for the Document Palette, saved.

Colours in the Document palette (as shown in the Swatch tab) are just saved locally, along with the drawing's current defaults. That is, the colours don't automatically carry over to new drawings. However changes to the other palettes are saved globally, in that colour changes will carry over to new documents automatically.

To load a named palette:

1. In the Swatch tab, click the down arrow on the ![Palettes icon] **Palettes** button.

2. From the resulting drop-down menu, select an Standard RGB, Standard CMYK, or "themed" palette, or a palette that you've created yourself.

The loaded palette's colours appear as swatches in the Swatch tab, replacing the swatches previously visible.

To create a new custom palette:

1. With ![icon] ▼ **Palettes** selected in the Swatch tab, click the ▷ **Tab Menu** button in the tab's top right-hand corner and choose **Add New Palette...**.

2. Enter a name for the new palette and click **OK**. The new empty palette is displayed and its name will appear in the Palettes drop-down menu.

To delete a new custom palette:

1. In the Swatch tab, select the palette for deletion from the ![icon] ▼ **Palettes** drop-down list.

2. Click the ▷ **Tab Menu** button in the top right-hand corner and choose **Delete Palette...**. After confirmation, the palette is removed from the list.

To save the current Document Palette:

1. Right-click anywhere in the Document Palette and choose **Palette Manager...**.

2. In the dialog, choose the **Options** button, pick **Save Palette As...** and save the palette to a new .PLT file.

> If you store the file in another folder to the initially prompted one, then your saved palette will not appear in the **Palettes** drop-down menu.

Working with gradient fills

Gradient fills are those that use gradients—small "spectrums" with colours spreading between at least two defined **key** values. Specifically, gradient fills include the **Linear**, **Radial**, **Ellipse**, **Conical**, **Square**, **Three Colour**, and **Four Colour** types. Once you've applied a gradient fill to an object using the Swatch tab (see Setting fill properties on p. 143), you can use the **Fill Tool** to edit the object's **fill path**, defining the placement of the spectrum across the object.

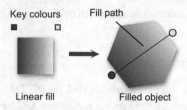

Key colours

Fill path

Linear fill

Filled object

Applying a gradient fill

There are several ways to apply a gradient fill as a line colour or object fill: using
the Fill Tool or via the Swatch tab . Using the Fill Tool, you can vary the fill's
path on an object for different effects.

To apply a gradient fill (Fill Tool):

1. Select a coloured object.

2. Click 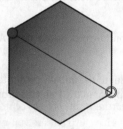 **Fill Tool** on the **Drawing** toolbar.

3. Click and drag on the object to define the fill path (a solid line). The
   object takes a simple Linear fill, grading from the current colour of the
   object, ending in white (objects filled with white will grade from white
   to black, to show contrast).

To apply a gradient fill (Swatch tab):

1. Select an object.

2. Click the Swatch tab and ensure the **Fill** swatch is placed in front of
   Line swatch.

3. Select the [ ] ▼ **Gradient** button's drop-down menu and pick a
   gradient category.

4. Click the thumbnail for the fill you want to apply.

- or -

Drag from the gallery swatch onto any object.

Editing the fill path

If an object using a gradient fill is selected, you'll see the **fill path** displayed as one or more lines, with circular nodes marking where the spectrum between each key colour begins and ends. Adjusting the node positions determines the actual spread of colours between nodes. You can also edit the fill by adding, deleting, or changing key colours.

To adjust the gradient fill path on a selected object:

1. Select an object with a gradient fill.

2. Click ![Fill Tool icon] **Fill Tool** on the **Drawing** toolbar. The object's fill path appears.

3. Use the Fill Tool to drag the start and end circular path nodes, or drag on (or outside) the object for a new start node, creating a new fill path as you drag. The gradient starts where you place the start node, and ends where you place the end node.

4. To constrain the fill path in 15-degree increments, hold down the **Shift** key while dragging. On Ellipse fills, **Ctrl**-constraining also forces the gradient's aspect ratio to match the object's bounding box.

Each gradient fill type has a characteristic path. For example, Radial fills have single-line paths, with the gradient initially starting at the object's centre. Ellipse fills likewise begin at the centre, but their paths have two lines so you can adjust the fill's extent in two directions away from the centre. Radial fills are always evenly circular, while Ellipse fills can be skewed in one direction or another.

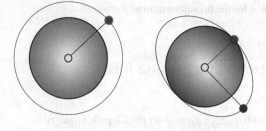

Radial Fill   Ellipse Fill

Experiment to discover new effects! For example, you
can widen or narrow the gradient's extent, even drag
either node completely outside the object. Or, for a
Radial fill on a round shape, try placing the start node
near the figure's upper edge, off-centre, to create a
reflection highlight.

For details of how to edit and manage gradient fills, see online Help.

Editing the fill spectrum

Whether you're editing a fill that's been already been applied to an object, or
redefining one of the gallery fills, the basic concepts are the same. Whereas solid
fills use a single colour, all gradient fills utilize at least two "key" colours, with a
spread of hues in between each key colour, creating a "spectrum" effect.

You can either edit the fill spectrum directly using the **Fill Tool** or use
Format>Fill (to access the Gradient Fill Editor dialog). With the Fill Tool
selected, colours can be selected from the Studio's Colour or Swatch tab to
replace a selected node's colour, or dragged from the Swatch tab to create new
nodes on the fill path). Both methods let you define key colours. The Fill Tool
method is more convenient for this, but with the dialog you can also fine-tune
the actual spread of colour between pairs of key colours.

The editing of gradient fills is a complex operation and is covered in greater detail in the online Help.

Working with bitmap and plasma fills

A **bitmap fill** uses a named bitmap—often a material, pattern, or background image. DrawPlus supplies an impressive selection of preset bitmap fills on the Swatch tab, and you can import your own.

A **plasma fill**, sometimes called a fractal fill, is a bitmapped pattern with dark and light regions, useful for simulating cloud or shadow effects. Again, the Swatch tab hosts a selection of these fills.

Once you've applied either type of fill to an object using the Swatch tab (see Setting fill properties on p. 143), you can adjust the fill's tint with the Shade/Tint slider in the Colour tab (use Display mode drop-down menu), and use the Fill Tool to edit the object's **fill path**, defining the placement of the fill across the object.

Editing the fill path

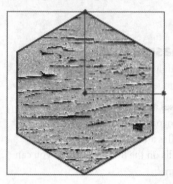

If an object using a bitmap fill is selected, you'll see the **fill path** displayed as two lines joined at a centre handle. Nodes, shown as small filled circles, mark the fill's centre and edges.

To reposition the fill's centre, drag the centre handle. To create a skewed or tilted fill region, drag one or both edge nodes sideways.

Unlike the other fill types, bitmap and plasma fills don't simply "end" at the edges of their fill path. Rather, they **tile** (repeat) so you can fill indefinitely large regions at any scale. By dragging the edge nodes in or out with the Fill Tool, you can "zoom" in or out on the fill pattern.

For details of how to edit and manage bitmap and plasma fills, see DrawPlus help.

Changing bitmap gallery fills

The bitmap gallery on the Swatch tab provides a large selection of bitmaps, grouped into categories like Abstract, Material, Patterns, and so on. The existing categories are already populated with preset swatches, but initially, there's one category ("My Bitmaps") that's empty and reserved for your own bitmaps. You can add more categories, and add bitmaps to them either by importing directly from a file or by adopting the bitmap fill of an object on the DrawPlus page. See online Help for more information.

Working with mesh fills

A **mesh fill** works like a gradient fill but uses a more complex fill path, with a grid or "mesh" of many nodes representing separate key colours. The overall effect, especially useful for multifaceted highlighting, arises from the colour gradients that spread between each of these nodes.

As an example, the **Mesh Fill Tool** (applied below right) can be used to dramatic effect on a sports car's bodywork. With the tool enabled, a mesh of editable patches and nodes are revealed.

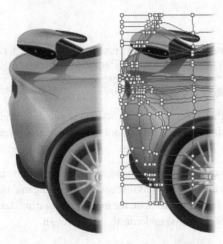

A mesh fill is applied to an object via the Swatch tab's Gradient gallery (see Setting fill properties on p. 143). You can edit the mesh itself with the Mesh Fill Tool and the accompanying context toolbar to achieve unique results. The path lines that connect nodes in a mesh fill are actually curves, so editing the mesh is similar to the method for Editing lines and shapes. Simple warping effects, colour spread changes and path line curvature can all be affected. The tool lets you reshape curved path lines by adjusting one or more nodes and their control handles. In addition, the areas between four nodes called "mesh patches" can be recoloured or moved individually or in multiples. As for curved lines you can add, delete, and move one or more nodes at any time.

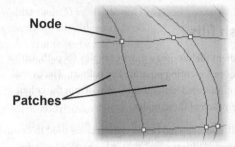

For details of how to edit and manage mesh fills, see online Help.

Setting opacity

> 💡 **Key point!** In DrawPlus, opacity is a property of colour; both can be set in the Colour tab in combination. Transparency refers to object-based gradient or bitmap transparency effects, set via the Transparency tab or Transparency Tool.

Opacity is great for highlights, shading and shadows, and simulating "rendered" realism. It can make the difference between flat, ordinary visuals and sparkling realism!

Opacity in the inverse of transparency—fully opaque (100%) is no transparency (0%), and vice versa. It works rather like fills that use "disappearing ink" instead of colour. The less opacity in a particular spot, the more "disappearing" takes place there, and the more the object(s) underneath show through.

The **Opacity** slider (Colour tab) can be used to alter the opacity of a specific colour, whether that colour is a solid fill (in an object or on a line), or a node's colour on a gradient fill path. Opacity can be applied locally to each object; the default is 100% opacity, i.e. the object is fully opaque.

For solid fills, the opacity change will be made uniformly across the object's interior (see below). For gradient fill paths, different opacity levels can be assigned with colour along the fill path. The combination of different colours and semi-transparency allow interesting colour blends to be made.

| 100% opacity (solid fill) | 50% opacity (solid fill) | 100%-0%-100%-0%-100% opacity (gradient fill path) |

Reducing the opacity on solid fills creates a blend between upper and lower object colours. Similarly, more complex colour blends occur along a gradient fill path when points along the path (called nodes) have reduced opacity settings.

> ✦ Gradient fill paths are explained in detail in *Working with gradient fills* on p. 155.

> ✦ Don't get confused between fill paths and transparency paths. The former is referred to here, but the latter is used to apply different levels of transparency along a transparency path instead of colour.

To apply solid opacity:

1. Select the object(s) and display the Studio's **Colour tab**.

2. Drag the slider to the left for a reduced opacity setting (e.g., 20%); drag right to increase opacity. This makes objects appear semi-transparent, or if set to 0%, fully transparent.

To apply solid opacity (to a fill path):

1. Select the object(s) and display the Studio's **Colour tab**.

2. Click **Fill Tool** on the **Drawing** toolbar.

3. Click on any displayed node along the fill path. Use **Shift**-select for selecting multiple nodes.

4. From the Colour tab, drag the slider to the left for a reduced opacity setting. You'll notice the new opacity setting influencing the fill's appearance (if placed in front of another coloured object).

Using transparency effects

While uniform opacity can be applied along with colour via the Colour tab (see Setting opacity on p. 162), it's possible to apply gradient transparency via the **Transparency tab** or **Transparency Tool independent** of colour. Bitmap transparency can also be applied exclusively via the Transparency tab.

Just as a gradient fill can vary from light to dark, a gradient transparency varies from more to less transparency, i.e. from clear to opaque. Picking a linear transparency preset from the Transparency tab, and applying it to a hexagonal shape, shows the transparency effect.

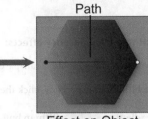

Path

Linear
Transparency

Effect on Object

Transparency can also be applied along a custom drawn transparency path using the Transparency Tool, in the same way as the equivalent fill path (see p. 156). Transparency paths are easily editable.

> ★ Transparency effects are applied locally to each object. Applying different transparency effects won't alter the object's fill settings as such, but may significantly alter a fill's actual appearance.

Applying transparency effects

There are two ways to apply transparency effects, i.e. via the:

- Transparency tab

- Transparency Tool

Let's check out the Transparency tab. As with the Swatch tab, there are galleries for both gradient and bitmap transparencies.

Gradient transparency galleries include **Linear** (opposite), **Radial**, **Ellipse**, **Conical**, **Plasma**, **Square**, **Three Points** and **Four Points**, ranging from clear to opaque.

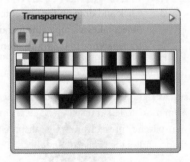

The **Bitmap** transparency gallery hosts texture maps based on the Swatch tab's selection of bitmaps.

Each preset's tooltip identifies its

category.

To apply gradient or bitmap transparency effects:

1. With your object selected, go to the Transparency tab.

2. For gradient or bitmap transparency, click the drop down arrow on the ▾ **Gradient** or ▾ **Bitmap** button, respectively. Select a category from the flyout, then click a thumbnail in that category.

   - or -

   Drag the desired thumbnail from the gallery to an object.

3. The transparency is applied to the object(s).

★ Sometimes objects of a lighter colour will not display their transparency clearly—ensure the transparency is applied correctly by temporarily placing the object over a strong solid colour.

To apply gradient transparency with Transparency Tool:

1. Select an object.

2. Click ▢ **Transparency Tool** on the **Drawing** toolbar.

3. Click and drag on the object to define the transparency path. The object takes a simple linear transparency, grading from 100% transparency to 0% transparency in the direction you drag.

You've freeform control over where the path starts and ends, and the direction in which the path will be drawn. You can even click again to redraw the path.

Editing gradient transparency

Once you've applied a transparency, you can adjust its **path** on the object, and the **level** of transparency along the path. You can even create more complex transparency effects by adding extra nodes to the path and assigning different levels to each node.

> 💡 You cannot alter the values in a bitmap transparency.

To adjust the transparency path directly:

- Use the Transparency Tool to drag individual nodes, or click on the object for a new start node and drag out a new transparency path. The effect starts where you place the start node, and ends where you place the end node. For bitmap and plasma transparencies, the path determines the centre and two edges of the effect.

To edit transparency levels (via dialog):

For more advanced path editing, the **Gradient Transparency Editor** dialog can be used exclusively (this is similar to the Gradient Fill Editor).

The dialog lets you fine-tune the actual spread of transparency between pairs of key values, and displays the transparency gradient, with pointers marking the nodes (corresponding to nodes on the path) that define specific transparency values. Black represents 100% opacity, and white represents 0% opacity, with greyscale values in between. A sample window at the lower right shows the overall transparency effect.

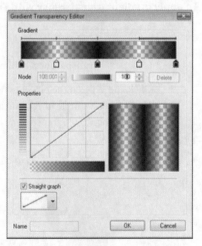

For details of how to edit and manage transparency, see online Help.

Working with Pictures

9

Importing pictures

Pictures that can be imported into DrawPlus can belong to one of two groups:

- **Bitmapped** pictures, also known as **bitmaps** or **raster** images, are built from a matrix of dots ("pixels"), rather like the squares on a sheet of graph paper. They may originate as digital camera photos or scanned images, or be created (or enhanced) with a "paint" program or photo editor. As with other object fills, you can add these bitmaps to the Bitmap fill gallery to be used as fills for other objects. For details, see Changing bitmap gallery fills on p. 160.

- **Vector** graphics, are resolution-independent and contain drawing commands such as "draw a line from A to B." These are like DrawPlus drawings, made of many individual objects grouped together, and you can edit them in the same sort of way. You have the choice of ungrouping the objects in order to edit them further, or leaving them as a group. Vector graphics such as **Windows MetaFiles** (.wmf) and **Serif MetaFiles** (.smf) can be imported; both combine raster and vector information, the latter being Serif's proprietary metafile format (great for sharing between Serif applications).

Any imported picture ends up as an object you can select, move, scale, shear, rotate—and even cut or crop using the **Knife** or **Crop Tool** on the **Drawing** toolbar.

To import a picture from a file:

1. Click ![Insert Picture icon] **Insert Picture** on the **Drawing** toolbar.

2. From the dialog, locate and select the file to import, then click **Open**.

   The dialog disappears and the mouse pointer changes to the ![Picture Size cursor] Picture Size cursor. What you do next determines the initial size, placement, and aspect ratio (proportions) of the picture.

3. Either:

   - To insert the picture at a default size, simply click the mouse.
   - or -

- To set the size of the inserted picture, drag out a region and release the mouse button.

By default, the picture's aspect ratio is preserved. To allow free dragging to any aspect ratio, hold down the **Shift** key. To constrain the aspect ratio while scaling from the picture's centre as you drag, hold down the **Ctrl** key.

Notes:

- For importing from an inserted Kodak PhotoCD, choose **Picture>Photo CD...** from the **Insert** menu.

- Once placed, you can swap the picture with the [🖼 Replace Picture] button on the context toolbar.

- You can always resize a picture as required, after it has been placed, by dragging its handles. For the finer points of resizing, see Resizing objects on p. 120.

- For image adjustment, a Picture context toolbar appears automatically when you select an image on the page. You can adjust **contrast**, **brightness**, **contrast**, **Red Eye** or apply **Auto Level** or **Auto Contrast**. To fix image deficiencies, select the toolbar's **Image Adjustments** button. Image adjustments are made possible with a comprehensive mix of colour correction/adjustment tools. See DrawPlus help for further information.

- If you select an image with areas of transparency, you'll be able to manipulate the image's outline, i.e. convert to curves, apply line properties, effects, etc.

Importing camera and scanner images

In recent years, the increasingly more sophisticated image management software supplied with such digital devices means that DrawPlus leaves the photo management aspect of importing photos and images to the manufacturer's software (installed with the device on your computer). However, what DrawPlus will offer is the ability to choose between different TWAIN sources, launch the manufacturer's software automatically and subsequently place any chosen photos/images onto the DrawPlus page.

To set up your digital device for image acquisition:

- Follow the instructions supplied with the device.

> When acquiring images from a camera that appears in Windows as a Removable Disk, ensure that you follow recommended procedures for connecting and disconnecting the device.

To import pictures from a digital camera or TWAIN device (scanner):

1. If you have multiple TWAIN-compatible devices, choose the device from which your image will be acquired—**Picture>TWAIN>Select Source...** from the **Insert** menu lets you select your device from a menu.

2. For scanning or photo import, choose **Picture>TWAIN>Acquire** from the **Insert** menu to open the device's image management dialog. Follow the device manufacturer's instructions, and select the scanned image or photo for import.

3. In DrawPlus, the ⬛ Picture Size cursor is displayed which allows image/photo to be placed at default size (by single-click) or sized (by dragging across the page).

Using Image Cutout Studio

Image Cutout Studio offers a powerful integrated solution for cutting objects out from their backgrounds. Depending on the make up of your images you can separate subject of interests from their backgrounds, either by retaining the subject of interest (usually people, objects, etc.) or removing a simple uniform background (e.g., sky, studio backdrop). In both instances, the resulting "cutout" image creates an eye-catching look for your publication.

The latter background removal method is illustrated in the following multi-image example.

The white initial background is discarded, leaving interim checkerboard transparency, from which another image can be used as a more attractive background. A red tint on the second image's background is used to indicate areas to be discarded.

To launch Image Cutout Studio:

1. Select an image to be cut out.

2. Select ![Cutout Studio] from the displayed Picture context toolbar. Image Cutout Studio is launched.

> ★ Your original image, if linked, is unaffected in Image Cutout Studio. However, embedded images, when cut out, are altered permanently in the project.

Choose an output

It's essential that you choose an output type prior to selecting areas for keeping/discarding. Either an alpha-edged or vector-cropped bitmap can be chosen as your output type prior to selection. The choice you make really depends on the image, in particular how well defined image edges are. Let's look at the output types and explain the difference between each.

Use when cutting out objects with poorly defined edges. Transparency and pixel blending are used at the outline edge to produce professional results with negligible interference from background colours. The term "alpha" refers to a 32-bit image's alpha transparency channel.

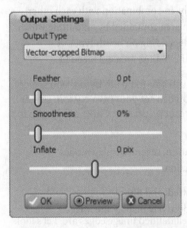

Use on more well-defined edges. A cropped image with crop outline is created which can be later manipulated with the crop tools. You can optionally apply feathering and smoothness to the image edge; the background colour will not be removed.

To create an alpha-edged bitmap:

1. Select **Alpha-edged Bitmap** from the **Output Type** drop-down menu.

2. Drag the **Width** slider to set the extent to which the "alpha" blending is applied inside the cutout edge.

3. Adjust the **Blur** slider to smooth out the cutout edge.

To create a vector-cropped bitmap:

1. Select **Vector-cropped Bitmap** from the **Output Type** drop-down menu.

2. Drag the **Feather** slider to apply a soft or blurry edge inside the cutout edge.

3. Drag the **Smoothness** slider to smooth out the cutout edge.

4. The **Inflate** slider acts as an positive or negative offset from the cutout edge.

Selecting areas to keep or discard

A pair of brushes for keeping and discarding is used to enable parts of the image to be selected. The tools are called **Keep Brush** and **Discard Brush**, and are either used independently or, more typically, in combination with each other. When using either tool, the brush paints an area contained by an outline which is considered to be discarded or retained (depending on brush type). A configurable number of pixels adjacent to the outline area are blended.

> 💡 Either tool allows the default brush size to be set before you select areas for keeping/discarding. You can set your own custom size or use a small, medium, or large preset brush size. Choose from the top of the Studio workspace.

To aid the selection operation, several display modes are available to show selection.

Show Original, **Show Tinted**, and **Show Transparent** buttons respectively display the image with:

- selection areas only

- various coloured tints aiding complex selection operations

- checkerboard transparency areas marked for discarding.

For Show tinted, a red tint indicates areas to be discarded; a green tint shows areas to be kept.

For Show transparent mode, a different **Background colour** can be set (at the bottom of the Studio) while Show Transparent is enabled; this may help give better contrast at cut edges while fine tuning.

To select image areas for keeping/discarding:

1. In Image Cutout Studio, click either [image] **Keep brush** or [image] **Discard brush** from the left of the Studio workspace.

2. (Optional) Pick a **Brush size** suitable for the area to be worked on.

   Brush Size [icons] ⬆48 pix ▶

3. (Optional) Set a **Grow tolerance** value to automatically expand the selected area under the cursor (by detecting colours similar to those within the current selection). The greater the value the more the selected area will grow.

4. Using the circular cursor, click and drag across the area to be retained. It's OK to repeatedly click and drag until your selection area is made— you can't lose your selection unless you click the **Reset** button. The **Undo** button reverts to the last made selection.

5. If you're outputting an alpha-edged bitmap, you can refine the area to be kept/discarded within Image Cutout Studio (only after previewing) with Erase and Restore touch-up tools. Vector-cropped images can be cropped using standard DrawPlus crop tools outside of the Studio.

> Make your outline edge as exact as possible by using brush and touch-up tools before committing your work.

6. Click [✓ OK] to create your cutout, or [✗ Cancel] to abort the operation.

You'll see your image on the poster page in its original location, but with the selected areas cut away (made transparent).

Refining your cutout area (alpha-edged bitmaps only)

If a vector-cropped image is created via Image Cutout Studio it's possible to subsequently manipulate the crop outline using the Crop Tool. However, for alpha-edged bitmaps, Erase and Restore touch-up tools can be used to refine the cutout area within the Studio before completing your cutout. The latter can't be edited with crop tools.

> The touch-up tools are brush based and are only to be used to fine-tune your almost complete cutout—use your Keep and Discard brush tools for the bulk of your work!

To restore or remove portions of your cutout:

1. With your cutout areas already defined, click (Output settings tab). You can use the button to check your cutout as you progress.

2. Click the **Restore Touch-up Tool** or **Erase Touch-up Tool** button from the left of the Studio workspace.

3. Paint the areas for restoring or erasing as you would with the brush tools.

4. Click .

> If you've touched up part of your image between each preview, you'll be asked if you want to save or discard changes.

Autotracing

Instead of manually tracing a design, it's possible to automatically convert bitmaps back into vector objects by using **autotracing**. Its main function is for speedily reworking bitmapped **logos** (for further design modification), but its use is not confined to this. In fact, both greyscale and colour **photos** can equally be autotraced for eye-catching artistic effects.

For each of these uses, DrawPlus offers a studio environment and a specific **preset profile** which will produce optimum results while autotracing artwork of your chosen type. These profiles are called **Logo Image Trace**, **B/W Image Trace**, and **Photo Image Trace**.

- **Logo Image Trace**. For vector bitmaps (e.g., logos, signatures, or other designs with antialiasing).

- **B/W Image Trace**. For black and white photos and hand drawings.

- **Photo Image Trace**. For colour photos.

The autotracing process is performed in a studio environment, which makes use of the above profiles. The studio gives the opportunity to preview before tracing, and customize chosen profile settings further to your liking. Most profile settings are unique to the profile.

To autotrace a selected image:

1. Click the drop-down arrow on the [Auto Trace ▼] button (**Standard** toolbar) and select a profile from the menu.
   - or -

   Click [Auto Trace ▼] and choose a profile from the profile selection screen.

2. The AutoTrace studio appears with the original artwork displayed, along with adjustable sliders, a colour palette (logo profile only), or a collapsible preview window (photo profiles only) showing how your output will look once traced.

3. (Optional) Adjust the sliders at the right of the workspace (each unique to the profile used); your profile settings will be modified. If you want to save these modified settings you must save the changed profile to a new custom name.

4. Click [⚙ Trace] to trace your logo, photo, or other bitmapped artwork. It's best to keep clicking this button to update your main window after any adjustment.

5. (Optional) For fine-tuning your traced output, several options are possible:

   • For removing colours in traced logo output, select a detected palette colour and then **Remove Colour**.

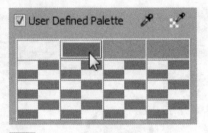

- You can **add** a new colour or **replace** an existing colour by dragging the **Colour Selector** to any colour on your computer screen. A respective empty or occupied colour swatch must be selected first. Remember to click **Trace** to refresh the view.

- Click **✻ Adjust** to access **Merge**, **Fill**, and **Node tools** for fine-tuning your vector output.

6. When you're happy with your traced output, click **✓ Accept** to add it to the page.

> All slider settings are described in full in the Help pane which accompanies the AutoTrace studio. Also covered are procedures for tracing greyscale and colour photos.

The autotracing procedure above differs slightly when applied to greyscale or colour photos, i.e. instead of comprehensive palette control you have a photo preview.

> Using photos in autotracing is covered in the tutorial "Cutting Out and Tracing."

Use the upper View toolbar for side-by-side previews and different outline views. The zoom controls at the bottom of the studio offer magnification and panning control.

Creating custom profiles

Adjusting any slider means that you've modified your chosen preset profile. If you want to keep the settings for future autotracing you can save the profile to a new name and reuse it from the drop-down menu (on the profile selection screen or within AutoTrace studio).

To save a custom autotrace profile:

1. Click **Save Current Profile**.

2. From the dialog, enter a custom profile name. The profile appears in the drop-down menu (in profile selection screen and studio).

To delete an autotrace profile:

1. Select the existing custom profile from the drop-down menu.

2. Click **Delete Current Profile**. The profile is removed from the menu.

Applying Special
Effects

10

Creating borders

The **Border Wizard** lets you create a border around the whole page or a selected object, or within a specific page region. It's possible to create your own border from a current object selection or from a preset border style.

To create a border:

1. (If creating a border around an object) Select the object first.

2. Select **Border Wizard...** from the **Insert** menu.

3. From the dialog, choose to select a border from a library of pre-designed borders (From library) or make your own border (based on the Current selection). Click **Next>**.

4. Choose where you want the border to be placed (e.g., Around the current selection) and click **Next**.

5. For presets, choose one of the pre-defined border designs from the scrolling list, and set the border's width. If making your own border, enable a different border style. The preview window shows what the border will look like in both instances.

6. Click **Finish**.

If you chose a whole-page or object border, it appears immediately. With the "custom" option, use the ⊹▣ cursor to drag out a region to be bordered.

> ★ You can create a border on individual pages but not on all pages simultaneously.

Creating blends

Blends enable you to "morph" any shape into any other shape via the **Blend Tool**. If the two shapes are separated in space, each step creates an intermediate shape, to create a kind of morphing effect where the colour, transparency, and line properties all change along with the object shape during the blend process.

The **Context toolbar** shown when the Blend Tool is selected also lets you adjust a number of blend settings before or after blending, i.e.

- the number of steps between the blend (to increase/decrease the smoothness of the blend)

- rate of transform via a set **Position Profile**

- rate of blend via **Attribute Profile**

- the **Colour Blend Type**

For more complex blending possibilities, objects can be multiply-blended (to/from other blends) to create truly stunning illustrations. It is possible to leap frog between separate shaped objects to create daisy-chained blends (by click and drag on each object consecutively).

To create a blend with the Blend Tool:

1. Select the  **Blend Tool** button on the **Drawing** toolbar.

2. (Optional) From the displayed Context toolbar, choose:

   - the number of "morph" Blend Steps to be taken between both points.

   - a Position or Attribute Profile for non-uniform blends. (See DrawPlus help).

   - a Colour blend type which defines how colour distribution occurs between the originating and destination object. You can Fade between colours by default, apply a Clockwise/Anti Clockwise colour spread around the HSL Colour Wheel (from the Colour tab), or use the Shortest or Longest route between colours on the HSL Colour Wheel.

3. Hover over the object to display the Blend cursor.

   ★ If blending to multiple objects, remember to group them in advance.

4. Click and drag the cursor, drawing a dashed line as you go, to your destination point (this must be on an object) and release. Your blend is created.

5. (Optional) Click the **Convert Blend Object into a Group Object** button on the context toolbar to group all blended objects.

⭐ Any blend can be modified at a later date via the context toolbar.

Creating rough edges

The **Roughen Tool** lets you selectively distort an object's outline, turning smooth-line edges into jagged outlines. The effect can lend cartoon-like flair to ordinary text or give QuickShapes an irregular appearance ...in fact apply it whenever it seems to suit the mood of the design.

To apply roughening:

1. Select an object and click 🌟 **Roughen Tool** on the **Drawing** toolbar.

2. Click on the object and drag up or down. The further you drag, the more pronounced the effect.

Adding drop shadows

You can apply commonly used drop shadows by using the **Shadow Tool**. When applied, the selected object is given a sense of depth (see rightmost moon).

The Shadow Tool offers freeform control of the drop shadow effect. With its on-the-page control nodes and supporting Shadow context toolbar, the tool offers various adjustments such as Opacity, Blur, and X (or Y) Shear.

Simple shadow
(drag from object centre)

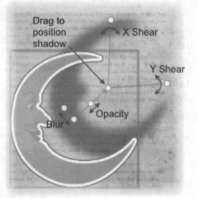

Offset shadow
(showing control nodes)

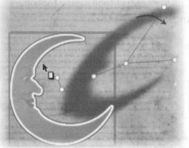

Skewed offset shadow
(adjusted X Shear)

> 💡 Once you've created a basic shadow, you can further edit it as needed using the Filter Effects dialog.

Applying drop shadows

1. Click the 🔲 **Shadow Tool** on the **Drawing** toolbar. You'll notice control nodes appear which allow adjustment as described in the annotated illustration above.

2. Drag across the object to create a drop shadow (note additional nodes being created).

3. Change blur, opacity, or shear accordingly with nodes (or via the displayed context toolbar).

To change a shadow's colour:

* Select the object, choose the **Shadow Tool**, then select a colour from the Studio's Colour tab.

To remove the shadow from an object:

* Double-click the object while the Shadow Tool is selected.

Applying 2D filter effects

You can apply some depth to your objects by applying an embossing effect.

* From the Effects tab, adjust the **Material Thickness** setting on your selected object. The greater the value, the greater the embossed effect.

Making feathered edges

Feathering applies a softer edge to your objects, such as embellishments or cut materials. The effect is especially useful for presenting a photo on the page.

* From the Effects tab, pick a **Feather Edge** setting. This is the distance inside the object's outline from which feathering will be applied.

The Feathering option in the Filter Effects dialog, offers independent control of **Opacity** and **Blur**, which can also be used in conjunction with other 2D filter effects.

For more advanced control of filter effects, DrawPlus provides a variety of **filter effects** that you can use to transform any object. The following examples show each filter effect when applied to the letter "A."

Drop Shadow	Inner Shadow	Outer Glow	Inner Glow

Inner Bevel	Outer Bevel	Emboss	Pillow Emboss

Gaussian Blur	Zoom Blur	Radial Blur	Motion Blur

Colour Fill	Feather	Outline

DrawPlus additionally provides the Shadow Tool for applying a shadow to an object directly on your page. Control handles let you adjust shadow blur, opacity and colour.

To apply 2D filter effects:

1. Click 🌟 **Filter Effects** from the **Drawing** toolbar. The Filter Effects dialog appears.

2. To apply a particular effect, check its box in the list at left.

3. To adjust the properties of a specific effect, select its name and vary the dialog controls. Adjust the sliders or enter specific values to vary the combined effect. (You can also select a slider and use the keyboard arrows.) Options differ from one effect to another.

4. Click **OK** to apply the effect or **Cancel** to abandon changes.

Creating outlines

DrawPlus lets you create a coloured outline around objects, especially text and shapes (as a **filter effect**). For any outline, you can set the outline width, colour fill, transparency, and blend mode. The outline can also take a gradient fill, a unique **contour** fill (fill runs from the inner to outer edge of the outline width), or pattern fill and can also sit inside, outside, or be centred on the object edge.

As with all effects you can switch the outline effect on and off. You'll be able to apply a combination of 2D or 3D filter effects along with your outline, by checking other options in the Filter Effects dialog.

Colour Fill

The **Colour Fill** effect applies a colour over any existing fill, and lets you achieve some effects that are not possible with other controls. For example, you can use Colour Fill to force everything in a complex group to a single colour, or recolour a bitmap in a solid colour (effectively ignoring everything but the transparency).

Feathering

Feathering is a filter effect that adds a soft or blurry edge to any object. It's great for blending single objects into a composition, vignetted borders on photos, and much more. You can apply feathering in conjunction with other filter effects.

> 💡 For simple feathering, use the Feather Edge setting on the Effects tab instead.

Blur

Various blur effects can be applied to DrawPlus objects. The types of blur include:

- **Gaussian**: the effect smooths by averaging pixels using a weighted curve.

- **Zoom**: applies converging streaks to the image to simulate a zoom lens.

- **Radial**: applies concentric streaks to the object to simulate a rotating camera or subject.

- **Motion**: applies straight streaks to the object to simulate the effect of camera or subject movement.

Using 3D filter effects

3D filter effects go beyond 2D filter effects (shadows, bevel, emboss, etc.) to create the impression of a textured surface on the object itself. Keep in mind is that none of these 3D effects will "do" anything to an unfilled object—you'll need to have a fill there to see the difference they make!

The Studio's Effects tab is a good place to begin experimenting with 3D filter effects. Its multiple categories each offer a gallery full of predefined effects, using various settings.

There you'll see a variety of remarkable 3D surface and texture presets in various categories (Glass, Metal, Wood, etc.). Click any thumbnail to apply it to the selected object. Assuming the object has some colour on it to start with, you'll see an instant result! Note that none of these effects will work on objects using the "Instant 3D" effect as described in the next section. Nor will they "do" anything to an unfilled object—you'll need to have a fill there to see the difference they make!

Alternatively, you can customize an Effects tab preset, or apply one or more specific effects from scratch.

To apply 3D filter effects from scratch:

1. Click **Filter Effects** on the **Drawing** toolbar.

2. Check the **3D Effects** box at the left. The **3D Lighting** box is checked by default.

> ✔ 3D Effects
>   3D Bump Map
>   Function
>   Advanced
>   2D Bump Map
>   3D Pattern Map
>   Function
>   Advanced
>   2D Pattern Map
>   Reflection Map
>   Transparency
> ✔ 3D Lighting

- **3D Effects** is a master switch for this group, and its settings of **Blur** and **Depth** make a great difference; you can click the "+" button to unlink them for independent adjustment.

- **3D Lighting** provides a "light source" without which any depth information in the effect wouldn't be visible. The lighting settings let you illuminate your 3D landscape and vary its reflective properties.

Check other 2D/3D Bump and Pattern Maps, Reflection Maps, and Transparency for mixed effects.

You can also store an object's customized effect on the Studio's Effects tab to use later.

For more information about creating and storing 3D filter effects, see online Help.

Applying paper textures

Use **paper textures** for a natural "paper-like" appearance on your design. Simulate textures of varying roughness and "feel" by selection of various real media textures such as **Canvas**, **Cartridge**, **Embossed**, **Parchment**, and **Watercolour**. As a paper texture is applied to all objects on a specific layer you can apply different paper textures on a layer-by-layer basis.

To apply a paper texture:

1. In the **Layers tab**, decide on which layer you wish to apply a paper texture to its objects.

2. Click the ▢ **Paper Texture** button shown after that chosen layer's name and, from the dialog, select the **Paper Textures** category. A gallery of texture thumbnails is displayed.

3. Choose one of the thumbnails and adjust percentage **Scale** and **Opacity** if needed.

4. Click **OK**. The button will change to indicate that a paper texture has been applied, e.g. ▣. Existing or any subsequently new objects will adopt the paper texture once applied.

To remove a paper texture:

1. Click the ▢ button on the layer from which you want to remove a paper texture.

2. From the dialog, simply click the **Remove** button. The paper texture is removed from all objects on the layer.

You can also swap or remove paper textures from within the Layer Properties dialog (right-click on a layer entry and choose **Layer Properties...**).

Applying dimensionality (Instant 3D)

Using the **Instant 3D** feature, you can easily transform flat shapes (shown) and text into three-dimensional objects.

DrawPlus provides control over 3D effect settings such as:

- **bevelling**: use several rounded and chiseled presets or create your own.

- **lighting**: up to eight editable and separately coloured lights can be positioned to produce dramatic lighting effects.

- **lathe effects**: create contoured objects (e.g., a bottle cork) with user-defined lathe profiles and extrusion control.

- **texture**: control how texture is extruded on objects with non-solid fills.

- **viewing**: present your object in three dimensions.

- **material**: controls the extent to which lighting has an effect on the object's surfaces (great for 3D artistic text!).

An always-at-hand 3D context toolbar hosted above your workspace lets you configure the above settings—each setting contributes to the 3D effect applied to the selected object. For on-the-page object control you can transform in 3D with use of an orbit circle, which acts as an axis from which you can rotate around the X-, Y-, and Z-axes in relation to your page. Look for the cursor changing as you hover over either the circles' nodes or periphery.

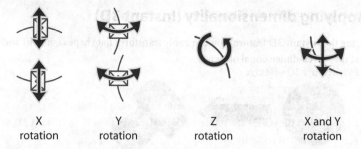

| X | Y | Z | X and Y |
| rotation | rotation | rotation | rotation |

Remember to take advantage of the hover-over cursor text or hintline which indicate the object's rotation currently or rotation while the operation is in progress, respectively.

> ★ Transform about your 3D objects' axes instead of your pages' axes by holding the **Ctrl** key down as you transform.

You can also adjust the angle and elevation of each "active" light on the page by dragging the light pointer to a position which simulates a light source.

To add dimensionality:

1. Select an object and click 🔲 **Instant 3D** on the **Drawing** toolbar.

   The object immediately adopts 3D characteristics with an orbit circle displayed in the object's foreground. You'll also notice a 3D-specific context toolbar appear above your drawing.

2. Click a 3D effect category from the first drop-down menu on the 3D context toolbar (from **Bevel**, **Lights**, **Lathe**, **Texture**, **Viewport**, **Material**); the other toolbars' options change dynamically according to the category currently selected. See online Help for more details.

3. Set each drop-down menu or input box for each category in turn. A little experimentation is advisable.

4. Hover over the object's orbit circle and rotate about the X, Y or Z axis (or X and Y axes together) by dragging about the circle's periphery (depending on the currently displayed cursor).

To revert your Instant 3D transform:

- Click Reset Defaults on the context toolbar.

To switch off 3D effects:

- Click Remove Instant 3D on the context toolbar. You can always select the object again then click the **Drawing** toolbar's **Instant 3D** button to reinstate the effect.

The Bevel and Lathe categories offer several presets that you can apply as your profile. You can also define your own custom profiles for both bevel and lathe effects from the Instant 3D context toolbar. (See online Help for more details.)

Applying Pseudo 3D

Pseudo 3D produces a object projection to follow one of three separate planes (top, front or right), either by using an **Isometric projection** (default) or other more complex projection. By bringing together transformed objects on each plane you produce the illusion of working in three dimensions, from a simple cube (below) to more complex 3D shapes, text, etc.

Each projection, from the same Quick Square object, can be presented as follows (with a combined multi-object cube).

| Top Plane | Front Plane | Right Plane | Combined cube |

 In DrawPlus, you can specify a plane (Top, Front, or Right) directly from the **Standard** toolbar's **3D Planes** flyout. While working with the toolbar all newly created objects will be drawn according to the currently set plane. Only one plane can be set at any one time.

For more complicated projections, DrawPlus also allows **Cabinet Oblique**, **Cavalier Oblique**, and various **Dimetric** and **Trimetric** projections to be applied; you can also design your own **Custom** projection. All projections represent a different object position about the X, Y and Z axes. Here's some simple cubes to illustrate a simple isometric projection compared to some more advanced projections.

Isometric	Dimetric1	Trimetric 1
(30,90,30)	(37,90,37)	(12,90,23)

Notice how the displayed angles on each of the above projections are shown after each name.

Practically, projection drawing can be challenging as it's sometimes difficult to visualize objects that appear three dimensional. To aid drawing, you can use the snapping grid which, when enabled, shows an alignment grid in the page background which intelligently switches to the current plane that you're working on. Whichever plane is set, drawn objects will then snap to the grid on the same plane.

To apply a Pseudo 3D projection:

1. From the **Standard** toolbar, click [3D Planes ▼], then select **Top Plane**, **Front Plane**, or **Right Plane** to set the plane to work on. (You'll see the snapping grid appear which reflects the currently set plane.)

2. Click a drawing tool and drag out the object (e.g., a Quick Rectangle) on the plane (an isometric projection is created by default).

3. All subsequently drawn objects are projected onto the currently set plane, unless it is swapped to a different plane (select a different button and draw a new object).

If this step-by-step process is followed, it's possible to bring together projected objects to create a larger object which simulates 3D characteristics.

> 🟊 You can remove any Pseudo 3D projection by selecting **No Projection** from the [3D Planes ▼] drop-down menu.

From the same drop-down menu, **Switch Plane on Select** can be disabled to stop automatically switching to the plane of a projected object when selected.

If you're creating a large number of objects, all on different planes, you can select all objects which project onto the same plane—useful for changing the colour of object faces for instance.

Selecting objects on the same plane:

*   From the **Select All On Plane** option on the **Edit** menu, choose **None**, **Top**, **Front**, or **Right** from the menu.

To project an object to a different plane:

*   Select a previously projected object, and with the **Ctrl** key depressed, choose a different plane from the [3D Planes ▼] drop-down menu.

Using Advanced Pseudo 3D

Up to now we've assumed that you've applied a default isometric projection. However, DrawPlus can create other axonometric projections by changing the current projection properties.

To apply an advanced Pseudo 3D projection:

1. Select the object.

2. Click **Projection Properties** on the [🔲 3D Planes ▼] drop-down menu.

3. From the dialog, select a projection type from the drop-down list.

> Isometric (30,90,30) ▼
> Isometric (30,90,30)
> Cabinet Oblique (0,90,60)
> Cavalier Oblique (0,90,45)
> Dimetric 1 (37,90,37)
> Dimetric 2 (16,90,37)
> Dimetric 3 (7,90,42)
> Dimetric 4 (15,90,15)
> Trimetric 1 (12,90,23)
> Trimetric 2 (5,90,30)
> Trimetric 3 (45,90,7)
> Trimetric 4 (54,90,17)
> Custom

Creating a custom projection:

*   From the **Projection Properties** dialog, pick a preset projection, and modify **Angle** and/or **Scale** values for one or more axes. The projection's name changes to **Custom**.

Saving a custom projection:

1. Click [💾] **Save**.

2. In the dialog enter a name for the new projection, and click **OK**. The entry will appear at the end of the drop-down menu.

Creating
Animations

11

Getting started with animation

What is animation? Like flip books, Disney movies and TV, it's a way of creating the illusion of motion by displaying a series of still images, rapidly enough to fool the eye—or more accurately, the brain. Professional animators have developed a whole arsenal of techniques for character animation—rendering human (and animal) movement in a convincing way.

A clear distinction has to be made between two types of animation techniques, both possible from within DrawPlus, i.e.

- **Stopframe animation**: also known as Stop motion animation, involves the animation of static objects frame-by-frame In the film industry, Stopframe animation is used within widely known productions based on figures made of clay or other bendable material (think King Kong!, and more recently Wallace & Gromit™ films (Aardman/Wallace and Gromit Ltd).

- **Keyframe animation**: performs movement of computer-generated objects from basic shapes to cartoon characters (used traditionally in Stopframe animation). Using the power of computing, smooth playback of animated objects is easily achieved between key moments in your animation, defined by the user as **keyframes**.

DrawPlus lets you export stopframe or keyframe animations to a variety of different formats. For more details, see Exporting animations (see p. 237).

For now we'll look at how to set up both Stopframe or Keyframe animation within DrawPlus.

To begin a new Stopframe or Keyframe animation (from Startup Wizard):

1. Start DrawPlus (or choose **File>New>New from Startup Wizard...** if it's already running).

2. Select **Create>Stopframe Animation** or **Create>Keyframe Animation** from the Startup Wizard.

3. From the Start From Scratch dialog, select a document category from the Documents pane (and a sub-category if applicable); categories are

optimized for the animation type. For custom sized pages, choose the **Custom Page Setup** button at the bottom of the dialog.

4. Select a document type thumbnail from the right-hand pane and click **Open**. The new document opens.

To begin a new Stopframe or Keyframe animation from scratch:

- Either:

    - Select **New>New Stopframe Animation** from the **File** menu.
    - or -

    - Select **New>New Keyframe Animation** from the **File** menu.

A new document window opens in the respective Animation mode.

To convert an existing drawing to either animation mode:

1. Choose **Convert to Stopframe Animation** or **Convert to Keyframe Animation** from the **File** menu. You'll be prompted to save changes (if any) to your existing drawing.

2. Select **Yes** to save your work, **No** to convert to an animation or **Cancel** to continue working on your current drawing.

To adjust the basic layout of your animation:

1. Choose **Page Setup** from the context toolbar (shown with Pointer or Rotate Tool selected).

2. Select a preset page type (e.g., Banner Ad) from the **Size** drop-down menu (or keep Custom selected, then set units for page width and height).

3. Choose **Wide** or **Tall** as the page orientation.

4. Choose values for left, right, top, and bottom **Margins**.

5. Click **OK**. Your page dimensions are expressed in pixels.

> You can modify page characteristics such as page size, orientation, number of pages, and snapping from the Pages context toolbar.

To save an animation:

- Choose **File>Save....** DrawPlus saves animation documents in the proprietary .DPA format (Drawings are saved as .DPPs).

Working with Stopframe animation

The most important difference in Stopframe animation mode to the usual Drawing mode is that you'll be working predominantly with the **Frames tab**, ideally suited for animation because of its width and easy control of individual frames (stopframes are spread along the tab for easier management).

Use the Frames tab exclusively to insert, delete, clone or reorder frames, and access individual frame properties. DrawPlus's **Hintline** toolbar navigation buttons let you jump to the first, previous, next, and last frames as you would for pages in normal documents. The tab also lets you preview the animation and enable onion skinning directly; exporting as a standalone animated GIF or video is carried out via the **File** menu.

The Frames tab is designed for Stopframe animation only, and only shows while in this mode. Don't get this tab confused with the Storyboard tab, used in the other type of animation supported by DrawPlus, Keyframe animation (see p. 213). Each tab hosts distinctly different tools suited to the respective animation type.

In most cases, your new Stopframe animation will have a single initial frame (e.g., Frame 1). To create new frames, you can either clone the current frame or insert a blank frame after the current frame. Choose to clone if you will be reusing the current frame's contents with a transformation of some kind (the most common way of simulating change or movement).

Try to think of your frame arrangement as a chronological sequence of static images which, when animated, will create the illusion of movement (like a cartoon flick-book). Once you've finished creating frames you can preview or export your animation, just as you would play the frames of a movie.

To view the Frames tab:

- Unless the tab is already displayed, click the ▬▬▬▬ handle at the bottom of your workspace to reveal the tab.

To clone the current frame to a new frame:

- Select a frame in the Frames tab, and choose **▦ Clone Frame**.

The frame is added after the selected frame.

> ★ Alternatively, use the Blend Tool to automatically create "intermediate" stopframes in steps between objects.

To generate a new blank frame:

- Choose **▦ Insert Frame** from the Frames tab.

Any new frame appears on the Frames tab to the right of existing frames, and then becomes the current frame. If you use the Frame Manager (accessible via right-click) you can choose to add frames before/after any existing frame.

To navigate between frames:

- Click on any visible frame to display its objects on screen (objects can then be edited).
  - or -

  Click the **First**, **Previous**, **Next**, or **Last** navigation button on the **Hintline** toolbar to jump to start/end frame and navigate frame-by-frame.

To rename a frame:

- Right-click a frame and choose **Properties...**. In the **Name** field, type in a new frame name. The new name is shown on the Hintline toolbar.

To change frame sequence:

- Drag the selected frame to a new position in the frame order. When the dragged frame's thumbnail creates a slightly wider space between two frames than usual, release the mouse button to place the frame to be moved.

To delete a selected frame:

- Click ⊗ Delete Frame from the Frames tab.

Onion Skinning

Onion skinning is a standard animation technique derived from cel animation, where transparent sheets enable the artist to see through to the preceding frame(s). It's useful for enabling precise registration and controlling object movement from frame to frame. You can turn the feature on or off (the default is off) as needed, and set the number of previous frames that will be visible (normally one).

To turn onion skinning on or off:

1. From the Frames tab, click the [Onion Skinning] button to turn onion skinning on or off.

2. To set previous frame to be visible, click [Properties], then set the number of frames in the **Onion Skinning** input box.

The preceding frame's objects will show behind those of the currently selected frame.

Previewing Stopframe animations

You can **preview** your animation prior to export at any time either directly from your Frames tab (shown in a Preview window) or from within your default web browser.

To preview in the Preview window:

- Click the [Preview] button on the Frames tab.

The animation loads into the Preview window and begins playing at its actual size and speed. Notice that you see only the drawn portion of the animation— any extra surrounding white space is cropped away. You can use the control buttons (Play, Stop, etc.) to review individual frames.

To preview in a web browser:

- For stopframe animation, select **Preview in Browser** from the **File** menu. The animation loads your default web browser and begins playing.

  This actually exports a temporary copy of the animation, using the current export settings and displays it in your web browser. You can leave the browser open and DrawPlus will find it again next time you issue the command.

Using background and overlay frames

DrawPlus supports two methods of reusing elements across multiple frames: **Background frames** and **Overlay frames**.

Background frames

You can designate any frame as a **Background frame**, which remains visible while the following frames animate "over" it.

To create a Background frame:

- In the Frames tab, click on the icon at the bottom of your chosen frame. You'll see the objects on the background frame carried forward either to the end of the animation or to the next background frame. Click again to revert back to a normal frame.

Overlay frames

The main advantage of frame overlaying is to save you the time of having to copy or redraw objects in a series where each frame builds cumulatively on previous frames. The white portions of **Overlay frames** become "transparent," so the contents of the preceding frame show through. The effect is cumulative, so overlays are most useful in a series where each frame builds on the contents of all the previous overlay frames.

> ★ The Overlay effect resembles that of onion skinning (see Working with Stopframe animation on p. 209), but it's actually a frame property that becomes part of the final animation.

To make the current frame an Overlay frame:

- In the Frames tab, click on the ⬚ icon at the bottom of your chosen frame. Click again to revert back to a normal frame.

> ★ You can make background and overlay frames by right-clicking a frame, and from **Properties**, enable Background or Overlay. Check the **Normal** radio button to revert the frame to a normal frame again.

Working with Keyframe animation

When compared with Stopframe animation (see Getting started with animation on p. 207), **Keyframe animation** offers a more powerful and efficient animation technology—it's a valuable time-saver as it saves having to declare every frame, letting your computer do the hard work! Essentially, the technique lets you create only user-defined **keyframes** through which objects animate, with each keyframe containing **Key objects** which can be assigned a position, rotation, attributes, etc. Intermediate steps between Key objects are created automatically and produce a smooth professional-looking inter-object transition (this is called **Tweening**); Tweened objects are created as a result. You won't see these intermediate steps showing tweened objects by default, but they exist transparently between key objects throughout your animation.

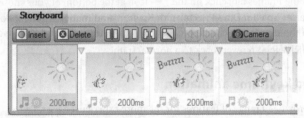

The Storyboard tab is the workspace for laying out your animation "story" in a chronological keyframe-by-keyframe sequence (from left to right). On export, your animation will play in this direction. Using the above "bee" animation in the tab illustration as an example, the bee is animated, while the sun and "Buzzzz" text remain static objects.

By adding objects (bee and sun) to a starting keyframe it's possible to automatically copy (or more correctly **run forward**) those objects forward when you create subsequent keyframes. This in itself doesn't affect animation, but it's the repositioning of a run forward object (such as the bee) in later keyframes that creates "movement."

Once keyframes are created, the animator has a great deal of control over how objects are run forward (or even backwards). You can introduce objects anywhere on the storyboard (so they appear for a limited time), and either run them forward or backwards by a specific number of keyframes (or right to the start or end of the storyboard). The "Buzzzz" text in the above example will only show from keyframes 3 onwards (i.e., from 6 seconds).

Supporting tabs

Other tabs supporting the Storyboard tab are exclusively used within Keyframe animation, i.e.

- The **Easing tab** is used for applying linear or non-linear changes between key objects with use of editable envelopes (e.g., to change object position, morph, scale, rotation, skew, colour, and transparency).

- The **Actions tab** allows objects and keyframes to be attributed actions which will run (e.g., go to a URL or designated marker) when an event is triggered (e.g., MouseOver, Rollovers, etc.).

> To set up your DrawPlus tabs for Keyframe animation mode, try one of the preset workspace profiles from the Startup Wizard (**Choose Workspace**).

Advanced keyframe animation

DrawPlus provides a range of features for the more experienced user, i.e.

- Apply actions in response to object events or at a specific keyframe either via an easy-to-use dialog or develop ActionScript™ code directly.

- Use the Keyframe camera for panning, zooming and rotation effects over keyframes.

- Masking lets you produce cutaways, i.e. punching through a layer(s) to reveal underlying objects.

- Add and manage sound and movies to enhance your animation. Manage files from one central location with the Media tab, which also allows viewing and direct replacement of media.

Getting started

> You can enter Keyframe animation mode via **File>New>New Keyframe Animation** or by converting your existing drawing by using **File>Convert to Keyframe Animation**.

Basic keyframe animations are created in a specific order:

1. Select a Page Setup from the context toolbar specific to your keyframe animation.

2. Create object(s), either static or for animation, on the page.

3. From the Storyboard tab, insert the number of keyframes and their duration via a dialog.

4. **Reposition** objects in subsequent keyframes to effect animation.

5. Export your keyframe animation as Adobe® Flash® (SWF).

Choosing a Page Setup:

1. Choose ⭐ Page Setup from the context toolbar (shown with Pointer or Rotate Tool selected).

2. Either:

   - For a custom document size, enter a Width and Height (in pixels) and set the orientation (Tall for portrait, Wide for Landscape). Ensure the Custom is set from the Size drop-down menu.
     - or -

   - For commonly used document sizes, select from the Size drop-down menu.

     Any document size can be changed for another via the supporting context toolbar.

3. (Optional) Under the **Background Colour** section, change the animation's background colour by clicking on the dialog-wide colour

swatch. The dialog lets you pick up a colour from a range of drop-down colour modes, your Document **Palette** or via a colour selector (drag and click anywhere on your computer screen to set). If you check the **Export transparent background to SWF** option, then any exported Flash SWF file will possess a transparent background (even if a background colour is set).

4. (Optional) **Animation Options** lets you increase/decrease the **Frame Rate** by dragging the slider left/right, respectively.

5. (Optional) To make your animation backward compatible to a specific version of Flash Player, set the **Flash Version** via the drop-down menu. Newer versions offer greater compression in exported Flash files.

6. (Optional) To reduce Flash file sizes, set the **Flash Bitmap Quality** to a lower percentage setting; this drops the resolution of placed bitmaps and any filter effects applied to objects.

7. Click **OK**.

★ Make use of the Startup Wizard's **Create>Keyframe Animation** or **Open>Design Template** options to choose preset page setups or Web Banner animation templates, respectively.

To view the Storyboard tab:

*   Unless the tab is already displayed, click the ▬▬▬▼ handle at the bottom of your workspace to reveal the tab.

We'll assume that you've drawn objects on the first keyframe. You can run forward these automatically throughout you animation by creation of additional keyframes—this builds up your animation "story" quickly. Other methods exist to run objects forward (and backwards) but let's concentrate on the insertion of keyframes to do this.

To insert keyframes:

1. From the Storyboard tab, select a keyframe and click ⬤ Insert .

2. From the dialog, choose the **Number of keyframes** to add to the Storyboard tab. Set a default **Keyframe duration** for each created keyframe.

3. Choose to add keyframe(s) at a **Location** before or after the currently selected keyframe or before/after the first or last keyframe.

4. (Optional) Check **Insert blank keyframes** if you don't want to include run forward objects in your keyframes. Blank frames are useful "filler" frames that add breaks in your animation for messages, logos, etc.

5. Click **OK**.

An inserted frame will honour any animation runs that may transect it if the **Insert blank keyframes** setting remains unchecked (by creating an additional tweened object). If checked, the blank frame will break any transecting animation path(s) and not add tweened objects.

Once you've created a keyframe sequence you can sub-divide or split any selected keyframe further.

To split a selected keyframe:

- Click the [ ] **Split keyframe** button on the Storyboard tab.

- From the dialog, enter the number of divisions that the keyframe is to be split into, then click **OK**. Each new keyframe's duration is an equal division of the original keyframe's duration.

To view or edit a particular keyframe:

- Select a keyframe in the Storyboard tab.
  - or -

- Click an object in an animation run that you know is associated with a specific keyframe (the keyframe will then be selected).

> ↖ Use your keyboard's **Page Up** and **Page Down** keys to navigate along your animation storyboard.

To delete a keyframe:

- Select the keyframe and choose [Delete].

Keyframe duration

Keyframe duration represents the amount of time in between each individual keyframe. The value is set according to how the keyframe was created, i.e.

- Inserting keyframes (blank or otherwise) lets you set the keyframe duration in an Insert Keyframes dialog (default 1 second).

- A splitting operation will create new keyframes whose duration will be a division of the selected keyframe's duration (by the number of keyframes to be split).

A keyframe's duration can be altered manually at any time.

To set the duration of an individual keyframe:

- Click the keyframe's duration (e.g., 1500ms) under its thumbnail, and, when selected, type a new value then click away.

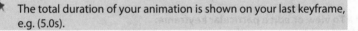

The total duration of your animation is shown on your last keyframe, e.g. (5.0s).

Storyboard control

Storyboard control is possible by using a selection of buttons grouped together on the Storyboard tab (equivalent options are on the **Storyboard** menu). They operate across the entire storyboard, as opposed to on an individual keyframe or key object.

⬜⬜ **Break storyboard**	Breaks the animation run that transects through a selected keyframe into two separate runs.
⬜◁▷⬜ **Compact storyboard**	A tool for tidying up your storyboard; any keyframes containing only tweened objects are removed from the storyboard.
◩ **Scale storyboard**	Expands or shrinks the whole storyboard. All keyframe durations are automatically adjusted to fit proportionally to the new **Scale** duration.

Adding sound and movies

Adding sound

To complement the visual effect of your keyframe animation it's possible to add audio. Sounds can be added either for the duration of a specific keyframe, or when an action is applied to an object event (see Applying actions on p. 228 for details on actions and events).

To add an audio clip:

1. On the Storyboard tab, click on the keyframe's 🎵 **Sound** icon (located below the frame's thumbnail).

2. From the dialog, navigate to your audio file, select it and click the **Open** button.

To remove a selected keyframe's audio clip, right-click and select **Clear Background Sound**.

Adding movies

As well as using sound in your keyframe animation, you can introduce movie clips. The movie is inserted into your chosen keyframe as an object which like any other object (QuickShape, Text, etc.) will need to be run forward for the movie to play throughout the animation.

DrawPlus supports various video formats including Flash Video (FLV), Flash SWF, AVI, WMV and MPG (MPEG1 and MPEG2), and QuickTime.

To add a movie:

1. Select the keyframe to which the movie is to be added.

2. Click [icon] **Insert Movie Clip** on the **Drawing** toolbar.

3. From the dialog, navigate to your movie file and select it.

4. Click **Open**.

5. Position the displayed [cursor] cursor where you want the movie to appear.

6. Either:

    *   To insert the movie at the movie's original size, simply click the mouse.

        - or -

    *   To set the size of the inserted movie, drag out a region and release the mouse button.

7. (Optional) Use the object toolbar controls to run forward/backward to the end/start of the storyboard (or by a set number of keyframes).

Previewing keyframe animations

You can **preview** your animation at any time either in a web browser or in Flash Player (Version 8.x is a DrawPlus install option). This is a quick way of checking it prior to export.

To preview:

- Click the down arrow on the ▷ ▼ button on the Storyboard tab, then choose to either:

  - **Preview In Browser....** The option displays a dialog which lets you preview in your web browser either standalone or by loading a target HTML page and associated SWF file (the target SWF file, e.g. a WebPlus banner, will be replaced by the animation to be previewed). Check Preview using existing HTML file for the latter, then navigate to and select HTML and SWF files.
  - or -

  - **Preview in Flash Player** (default). Use the navigation controls to review your animation as it would appear as an exported Flash SWF file. The animation loads Flash Player (if installed) and begins playing in a Flash Preview window.

Keyframe object control

We've just looked at storyboard control. However, a whole series of important **object control** tools are also available in keyframe animation. They are available on an **object toolbar**, displayed in-context under any selected object.

Initial grouped objects
show run forward, and
grouped object buttons

Objects along the animation run
show buttons for conversion to
key objects, object placement
and attributes.

The insertion of keyframes when you begin your animation will automatically run objects forward or backward. However, **Run Forward** and **Run Backward** commands let you introduce new objects in your animation which run across a limited number of keyframes or the entire storyboard.

To run object(s) forward/backward:

1. Select the keyframe which contains your chosen object.

2. Select the object, then click ▷▷ **Run forward** (or ◁◁ **Run backward** if on a later keyframe), located on the object toolbar directly under the selected object.

3. From the dialog, choose to **Run Length** either **To end of storyboard** or by **N Keyframes** (enter a number of keyframes to copy to). You can optionally run objects to the start or end of the storyboard, or by a set number of keyframes.

Once run forward or backward, you can move an object on any keyframe (normally the last) to make animation work. Objects that are not moved are called **tweened objects**, and show as transparent square nodes (see below) which are automatically created between any two **key objects**. If you move any of these interim tweened objects you change your animation to follow a non-linear path (see below)—as a result, the tweened object becomes a key object.

This takes care of repositioning objects, but what about changing an object's transform (morph, scale, rotation, and shear) or attribute (colour or transparency)? Simply, a selected tweened object can be modified just like any other object—it will be converted to a key object automatically as a transform or attribute change is applied.

> ★ 🔑 🔲 Use **Convert to key object** to lock a tweened object into place (by making it a key object). Use the opposite command, **Convert to tweened object**, to convert back to a tweened object (removing any repositioning, transforms, or attributes local to the object). Both options are on the object toolbar.

The Object toolbar also offers two commands for repositioning objects along the storyboard. **Update placement backward** updates a previous object's position to match the selected key or tweened object's current position. Conversely, **Update placement forward** updates later object's position accordingly.

To change object placement:

1. Select the object whose positional information you want to apply forward or backward.

2. From the object's toolbar, click either:

    *   ◁▯ Update placement backward to make a previous object's position match the selected object's position.
        - or -

    *   ▯▷ Update placement forward to do the same to later object positions.

3. From the dialog, choose to **Run Length** either to the beginning/end of the storyboard, or to a set number of keyframes before/after the currently selected object (choose the Run length drop-down menu, pick **N Keyframes** and enter a number of keyframes).

4. Click **OK**.

Like DrawPlus's Format Painter, you can also apply a specific object's attributes (colour, transparency, filter effects, shadows, etc.) to previous or later objects.

To change object attributes

1. Select the object whose attributes you want to apply forward or backward.

2. From the object's toolbar, click either:

   - The ◁ Update attributes backward button to apply attributes to previous objects.
     - or -

   - The ▷ Update attributes forward button to apply attributes to later objects.

3. From the dialog, choose to **Run Length** either to the beginning/end of the storyboard, or to objects a set number of keyframes before/after the currently selected object (choose the Run length drop-down menu, pick **N Keyframes** and enter a number of keyframes to copy to).

4. Click **OK**.

> You'll also find some useful options on the Run menu which can also be used to manipulate objects between keyframes or along the whole animation run.

Some other settings affect how objects animate along the animation run. These are hosted on the Easing tab and control object rotation, temporal tweening, natural motion, and how keyframes obey a Keyframe camera. The settings are applied between key object "segments" (and will apply until the next key object) or throughout the animation's run depending on the **Apply to Whole Run** check box setting (unchecked or checked, respectively). When the option is unchecked, objects can adopt different combinations of settings independently of each other, i.e.

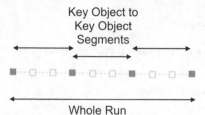

Key Object to
Key Object
Segments

Whole Run

To configure a "segment", select the first Key object ( ) then configure settings in the Easing tab (with Apply to Whole Run unchecked).

Clockwise Rotation	When checked, any rotation between objects is performed clockwise. Uncheck to rotate in an anti-clockwise direction.
Temporal Tween	Check to tween evenly between keyframes or over the whole storyboard (ignoring individual keyframe's time durations). Uncheck to honour any keyframe time durations. This is kept checked in most instances.
Natural Motion	When checked, animation occurs along a smoothed curving path through objects. Uncheck to animate along straight paths, with distinct "cornering" along the object's motion path.
Rotate on path	Check to allow an object (e.g., an arrow) to automatically rotate with changes of direction along an animation path. Uncheck for the object to follow the path but not to re-align to it.
Obey camera	If using the Keyframe camera feature, when the option is checked then a selected object will be panned or zoomed into. When unchecked, the object remains static, ignoring the camera. Use when text (company logo, a message, etc.) is to be permanently presented while panning and zooming is performed in the background.

Autorun

Although switched off by default, this advanced feature speeds up the animation process by automatically creating objects, their placement and attributes along the length of the storyboard, from a specific keyframe onwards. Even when editing an object, the changes are reflected throughout. Without Autorun enabled, objects are presented across keyframes by using the Insert button or clicking the object toolbar's **Run forward** or **Run backward** buttons.

★ The Autorun feature does not "autorun" objects backwards but instead only runs objects forward.

To autorun objects:

1. Click the ▷▷ Auto Run ▼ button on the Storyboard tab. The button is highlighted when enabled. Click again to disable.

2. Create or modify an object on a keyframe to see the effect on the object in subsequent keyframes.

As well as switching the Autorun feature on and off, you can also check one of the following options (click the down arrow on the Autorun button) to change how Autorun operates:

Creation and Placement	By default, an object will be created on every subsequent keyframe and object placement is mirrored throughout the subsequent keyframes of your storyboard.
Creation	The object is created on every subsequent keyframe throughout your storyboard but the object's position on keyframes remains unaffected.
Placement	The object's position is mirrored on subsequent keyframes on your storyboard.
Attributes	The attributes (colour, transparency, effects) of an object are mirrored to the same object on subsequent keyframes on your storyboard.

Applying actions (keyframe animation)

Selected objects can be assigned an event and corresponding **action**. The use of actions provides an interactive experience in response to a user's mouse up/down/press/release, key press/up/down, roll over, etc. As a typical example, an event such as a mouse press on an object can initiate an action such as a jump to a particular keyframe, e.g. an important point in your animation that could indicate contact details, important messages, etc.

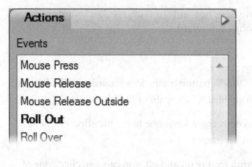

The Actions tab is used to apply actions to a selected object. By firstly selecting an event from the tab's Events scrolling list, you can then link that event to an available action—listed for selection within a single dialog, i.e.

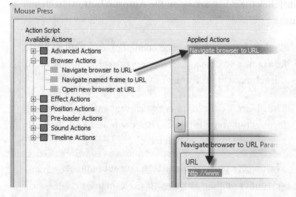

Actions are grouped into a tree menu structure whose categories include:

- **Advanced**: Begin/End blocks, apply conditions, create variables, variable control.

- **Browser**: navigate browser to URL (shown), navigate frame to URL Open browser with URL.

- **Effect**: named object control (hide, show, recolour).

- **Position**: move objects by pixel or to screen areas.

- **Pre-loader**: rewind animation, object stretch.

- **Sound**: increase/decrease volume, play/stop sound, set volume.

- **Timeline**: go to marker, animation frame, animation playback control (stop, play, rewind).

DrawPlus makes use of ActionScript, a language specifically designed for Adobe Flash applications, to allow a high level of interactivity between the exported Flash SWF and the user (e.g., a web visitor).

When an action is applied from the menu you may be prompted for a parameter setting (pixel width, colour, etc) but you can alter parameters at any time—without having to view underlying ActionScript code.

Optionally, a new action can be created from scratch within the dialog. Simply code directly or paste ActionScript into an Edit window.

To apply an action to selected object(s):

1. Select an object on any keyframe.

2. Double-click an event from the Actions tab.

3. From the dialog, navigate the tree menu, expanding the options if necessary, and click on a chosen action (e.g., Timeline Actions>Go to marker X).

4. Click the ⊳ button to apply the selected action (it moves across into the Applied Actions box), then repeat for optional additional actions. You may be presented with a dialog which prompts for object names or parameter values (colours, number of pixels, marker names, etc.) required for the underlying ActionScript code to act on.

5. (Optional) For multiple applied actions, you can order the Applied Actions list with the **Up** or **Down** buttons.

6. Click **OK**. You'll notice the selected event now shown in bold in the Actions tab.

The applied action can be edited by double-clicking the tab's bold event entry and, from the dialog, clicking the **Params** button (with object selected). To delete an action, use the **Delete** button to remove it.

We've looked at actions assigned to objects, but a keyframe can equally have an action associated with it. Especially useful on a starting keyframe, an Effect Action can be used to hide one or more selected objects before having them displayed on the second and subsequent keyframe (great for text introductions!). Actions are applied to keyframes via the **Frame Actions** dialog, which offers the same actions as those that can be applied to objects.

To apply action(s) to a keyframe:

*   Click on the ● icon under the keyframe's thumbnail.

The dialog displayed is identical to that used for actions applied to objects. Follow the above object actions procedure to apply actions to keyframes.

ActionScript, the underlying scripting language for actions, is normally hidden from the user in the above easy-to-use dialogs—you can view actions, their settings (as parameters), and select the action but generally not the underlying code driving it. However, the more experienced and/or adventurous can make use of a simple text entry system for developing ActionScript code from the same dialog.

To create custom ActionScript:

1. For a selected object, double-click an event from the Actions tab.
    - or -

    For a keyframe, right-click the keyframe and choose **Frame Actions**.

2. Click the **New** button to add a New Action entry to the Applied Actions list.

3. With the entry selected, click the **Edit** button. The Action Script Code Editor window is displayed.

4. Enter your ActionScript code either by coding directly or by pasting existing code in the window.

5. Click **OK**.

Click the **Flatten** button to rationalize several listed actions into one. A combined action named "Flattened Code" is created instead. Each code snippet will be run consecutively.

> ★ ActionScript Version 2 is supported in DrawPlus.

Creating markers

▽ Working in a similar manner to bookmarks, markers work along with actions, allowing jumps to particular keyframes on the storyboard. Markers are positioned between keyframes along the storyboard and need to be activated for use. Each marker can be named, which is especially useful for marker identification when you're using multiple markers along your storyboard. Additionally, a marker can be used to stop an animation, preventing your animation from looping—the **Stops playhead** marker setting will prevent the animation from continuing past that marker position.

To set a marker:

1. Click a ▽ marker icon after a chosen keyframe.

2. From the dialog, enter an easily identifiable **Marker Name**.

3. (Optional) Check **Stops playhead** to prevent your animation from continuing.

4. Click **OK**.

5. The marker's appearance will change accordingly, i.e.

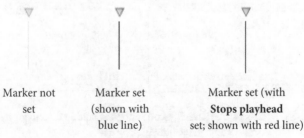

| Marker not set | Marker set (shown with blue line) | Marker set (with **Stops playhead** set; shown with red line) |

When used in conjunction with the Timeline Actions "Goto marker X" or "Goto marker X and stop" the exported animation can jump to different section according to a chosen object's event or the display of a keyframe.

Affecting change over time (keyframe animation)

DrawPlus uses the term **envelopes** to describe editable motion paths (or profiles) intended to define the rate of change (acceleration/deceleration) to an object's transformation or physical attributes (colour or transparency) in your animation run.

Envelopes are applied, created, modified and saved in the Easing tab. A series of envelope types can be applied between key objects in your animation or throughout the entire animation run. Typically, a non-linear **Position envelope** would alter how an object speeds up or slows down over the animation run. Other envelope types can alter the rate of transformation such as Rotate, Morph, Scale, and Skew.

You can manually edit any profile independently of each other such that you may have a mix of edited profiles and default linear ones. The Easing tab's **Envelope type** drop-down menu lets you select your envelope type, allowing you to then define a profile shape for that envelope in the pane. In most instances, an "All Envelopes" option can be used to affect a variable rate of change for **all** envelopes simultaneously.

The process or editing an envelope is identical, irrespective of envelope type. By default, any envelope is applied linearly (i.e., they change at a uniform rate over time) so you have to manually edit the envelope to apply a non-linear rate of change.

The differing rates of change of can be illustrated with a Morph Envelope between two simple QuickShapes.

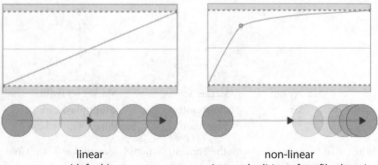

linear
(default)

non-linear
(manual editing of profile shape)

To apply an envelope:

1. Display the Easing tab.

2. Select an object from the Storyboard tab to which you want to apply the envelope.

3. Select a profile from the **Envelope type** drop-down menu (Easing tab). The displayed profile will be linear by default (see above), unless you've applied the envelope previously.

4. Pick a preset profile from the [⬛▼] drop-down menu below the profile window.

    - or -

    For a custom profile, hover over the turquoise line (the cursor changes to 🖰) and drag in any direction to position a newly created red node. Repeat the process for the number of nodes that you want to add to make up the profile. You can then fine-tune the profile shape by adjusting node positions accordingly.

    ★ Edit an existing profile from the preset drop-down menu to create profiles quickly.

DrawPlus will keep the applied profile unless you modify it or you reset the profile manually. If you'll be using the profile shape in the future you can save the current settings to your own saved profile.

To reset a selected envelope:

*   Click the [✖ Reset] button. The profile reverts to be linear (default).

To save your custom profile:

1. Modify the profile shape from an existing preset (or create from scratch).

2. Select **Add Easing Profile** from the Easing tab's ▷ **Tab Menu** button to save it. The new profile will appear at the bottom of the drop-down menu below the profile window.

To delete a profile preset:

1. Select **Manage Easing Profiles...** from the ▷ **Tab Menu**.

2. From the dialog, select the preset entry, click the **Delete** button, then click **OK**.

Keyframe animation tips and tricks

So far the emphasis has been on creating simple animations from scratch, keyframe/object control, and how change over time is affected.

In order to go one step further, and create more complex animations, you may want to explore more advanced features ranging from using Keyframe camera effects, applying masking effects, and changing an object's state.

Using the Keyframe camera

The camera effect lets you pan, zoom or rotate areas of your animation to create a more interesting visual appeal. Especially useful if you want to focus on parts of your animation (e.g., a main cartoon character or a company logo, telephone number, or web address), the feature is very powerful and should be used without making too many dramatic transformations (try zooming by small amounts over the animation duration).

To enable the Keyframe camera:

1. Select a keyframe to which you want to apply a pan, zoom or rotate operation.

2. To enable, click the 🎥 Camera button on the Storyboard tab. A single rectangular bounding box (shown with a solid blue border) is shown around the page which defines the visible area to be displayed. You'll notice a camera appear as a layer entry under the current layer in the Layers tab.

3. Reposition and/or resize the bounding box to set an initial view level that the animation can display.

4. (Optional) Set the bounding box in other keyframes, according to the desired effect. Otherwise a full screen view will be used in the remaining keyframes.

> 💡 With the camera enabled, select [📷 Reset Camera] on the object's toolbar to revert the display area back to the default.

For specific objects that are to ignore pan, zoom and rotation (think of a company logo which needs to remain static throughout the animation), with the object selected, uncheck **Obey Camera** on the Easing tab.

Masking

The option lets you mask one or more layers immediately below a purposely created mask layer. Mask layer objects cut away to reveal only underlying layer's objects showing under the mask object (the remainder is masked from view)—great for creating circular spotlights, keyhole shapes, or any other conceivable object shape. QuickShapes are ideal for this but don't discount using Artistic Text for interesting cutouts.

Try experimenting with a stationary mask layer with animation being performed on lower layers, animation on both mask and non-mask layers, or you could just animate the mask itself.

To create a mask:

1. With the Layers tab displayed, create a layer intended purposely for masking object(s), then place it directly **above** the layer(s) you want to mask.

2. Draw one or more objects on this mask layer. You can overlap objects but you won't need to combine the objects or worry about object fills (DrawPlus will work it out!). However, you might like to group multiple objects together.

3. (Optional) To mask multiple layers, double-click the mask layer and set the number of **layers** in the dialog's Attributes box.

4. (Optional) Run your selected mask objects forward and reposition them either at the end of the animation run or on a selected prior keyframe. This will allow the masked objects to animate.

5. Click the  **Mask** button to the right of the new mask layer's name (it then shows as Ⓜ).

6. To enable masking, click the adjacent 🔒 **Locked** button (this also locks the mask objects in place).

State behaviour

By default, any object drawn in DrawPlus is considered to be a **non-state object** (i.e., one that has a single set of attributes). Within Keyframe animation it's possible to convert such a non-state object to a **state object** by assigning it one or more "states" such as Normal, Hover, or Pressed, with each state possessing its own object attributes.

The advantage here is that in each state, the object can have a different appearance in response to a user event such as a mouse press or mouse hover over. This lets you creates interactive intelligent objects which change with your mouse movement/actions. Think of a "Play" button on your computer's music/video player having different appearance when clicked.

In DrawPlus, an object's state is indicated by its adjacent state buttons shown next to the object (only two states will be shown at any time; the third state is the current object's state).

For example, an object in Normal state shows adjacent ◉ **Hover** and ◉ **Pressed** buttons, i.e.

If you click either button you'll jump to that state's sub-object. If in Hover or Pressed state, you'll see the ◉ **Normal** button.

To convert to a state object:

1. Select the object.

2. Choose **State>Convert to state object** from the **Object** menu.

Use the **Convert to non-state object** from the same menu if you want convert back.

To change a sub-object's attributes:

- Click the state buttons to toggle between the different modes.

- Once in a chosen mode, modify the sub-object attributes (colour, transparency, effects, etc.) that will show for that mode (i.e., as **Normal**, on mouse **Hover**, or when the mouse is **Pressed**).

The use of state behaviours does not prevent you from assigning your own Actions to the different sub-objects. In fact, it's likely that you may want to show an object (e.g., a button) change colour on hover over, then jump to a URL on a subsequent mouse press.

Exporting animations

Exporting your stopframe or keyframe animation outputs your animation to a file which can be shared or viewed, either standalone or when included as part of a web page. DrawPlus lets you export to a variety of formats as indicated below:

Export	Stopframe	Keyframe
Flash SWF	✗	✓
Video	✓	✓
Image	✓	✓
CAD/CAM	✓	✗
Screensaver	✗	✓
Flash Lite/i-Mode	✗	✓

Flash SWF

The **Flash SWF** (ShockWave Flash) format has fast become the format of choice for interactive vector-based graphic animation for the web. Great for creating a simple or sophisticated animated toolbar for web page navigation, it is universally supported on web browsers. The files can be easily manipulated further (scaled, etc.) within Adobe® Flash®.

To export your animation as a Flash file:

1. Choose **Export>Export as Flash SWF...** from the **File** menu.

2. From the dialog, provide a ShockWave Flash file name and folder location, and click the **Save** button. You'll see an export progress dialog appear until the Flash file is created.

Video

Exported **video** formats include:

- **QuickTime**. The QuickTime video and animation format (**MOV**) developed by Apple Computer. It can be read on many platforms, including Microsoft Windows (needs QuickTime Player) and of course on Apple computers. QuickTime supports most encoding formats, including Cinepak, JPEG, and MPEG.

- **Serif Transparent Video**. The STV format is a useful proprietary format which can export animated text and logos with transparent backgrounds. The export benefits Serif MoviePlus users who would like to use their keyframe animation as an overlay (of titles, animated characters, etc.).

- **Video for Windows**. The Windows Audio Video Interleave file (**AVI**) is ideal for playback on a Windows computer. Defined by Microsoft, it supports different types of video, audio and image sequences in sync with a mono or stereo sound track along with compression (via a wide variety of codecs). AVIs are mainly for viewing on a computer. Appropriate codecs have to be installed on the computer.

- **Windows Media audio and Video**. The **WMV** format is best supported on PCs running Windows Media Player, although some other software even on other platforms can play WMV video. WMVs are Advanced Systems Format (.ASF) files that include audio, video, or both compressed with Windows Media Audio (WMA) and Windows Media Video (WMV) codecs.

- The **.GIF** format is ideal for web as it's universally supported by web browsers, and, as it's a multi-part format, it's capable of encoding not just one image but multiple images in the same file. A .GIF animation player or web browser can display these images in sequence, in accordance with certain settings (looping, frame delay, etc.) included in the file. The result—it moves! As with single-frame GIFs, if you opt to export your animation with the Transparency setting turned on, any unfilled regions of the graphic will become transparent in the GIF. All other regions will become opaque. Keyframe animation cannot export Animated GIFs. For details on using transparency in GIFs, see Using transparency effects on p. 164.

To export animation as video:

1. Choose **Export>Export As Video...** from the **File** menu.

2. From the displayed dialog's Basic tab, select your chosen export type from the **File type** and **Template** drop-down list according to the type of output video format you require.

3. (Optional) Click **Match project settings** to set an approximate video frame size based on your animation project's Page size (set in Page Setup).

4. Specify a name for file in the **Filename** box, clicking **Browse** and selecting a new location if you first wish to choose an alternate drive or folder to store your file.

5. (Optional) From the dialog's Advanced tab, make a new video template with the **Copy** button, then alter more advanced settings such as video Frame size (choose Custom then set a Width and Height), Pixel aspect ratio, Frame rate, Interlacing, Codec settings, and more, depending on the format to be exported. (See Exporting video (Advanced) in online Help for more details).

6. (Optional) Set an export **Quality**.

7. Click the **Export** button. Your project will then be composed and converted into the specified format and you will be shown a progress bar during this process.

Image

Within Stopframe animation, this option lets you create an animated GIF by default, which we'll focus on here. For keyframe animation, you can export a single keyframe as any type of image format.

To export as an animated GIF:

1. Choose [Export] from the Frames tab.

2. The Animated GIF format is pre-selected on the **Format** drop-down menu by default; if not, select it. If you choose another format, only the current frame will be exported. For full details on GIF export options, consult Exporting objects and drawings on p. 250.

3. Set a size for the GIF animation and whether it is based on the whole Page, Selected Area or Selected Objects. Leave the dpi setting at 96 for standard screen resolution.

4. On the **Animation tab**, which only appears in Stopframe Animation Mode, you can preview single frames or run the animation sequence, and make some final playback adjustments to the animation properties.

5. Click the **Export** button (or **Close** to simply record the settings if you plan to preview in a browser first).

6. Provide a file name and folder location, and click **Save**. Don't worry if you have extra white space around your image. Any unused border area will be cropped automatically, just as you saw in the Preview window.

Screensaver (Windows XP users only)

If you're working with keyframe animations, you also have the option of creating a screensaver file (.SCR). Your Windows XP-compatible exported file can be used on your computer (as for any screensaver file) or for distribution to friends and family equally.

To create a screensaver:

1. Choose **Export>Export as Screensaver...** from the **File** menu.

2. From the **Save As** dialog, enter a screensaver file name and save to C:\WINDOWS\SYSTEM32\ for the screensaver to be viewable and enabled.

3. In the next dialog, provide a title and contents for your screensaver's About box, then click the **OK** button.

4. Click the **Save** button. You'll see an export progress dialog appear until the screensaver file is created.

To enable the Screensaver:

1. Right-click on your Windows Desktop background and select **Properties**.

2. From the dialog, select the **Screen Saver** tab.

3. Select your screensaver from the **Screen Saver** drop-down list.

4. (Optional) Use the **Wait** input box to set an idle duration before your screensaver will be displayed.

Flash Lite/i-Mode

Use if you're intending to export a keyframe animation for mobile users operating mobile phones, personal organizers, and more. The format is optimized for viewing on smaller screen displays. The outputted file type is the same as that for Flash export, with a SWF file extension.

To export to Flash Lite/i-Mode:

1. Choose **Export>Export as Flash Lite/i-Mode...** from the **File** menu.

2. From the dialog, provide a ShockWave Flash file name and folder location, and click the **Save** button. You'll see an export progress dialog appear until the file is created.

Publishing and Sharing

Previewing the printed page

Print Preview changes the screen view to display your layout without guides, rulers, and other screen items. Special options, such as tiled output or crop marks, are displayed. Depending on your currently set printer's capabilities, your preview will show in either greyscale or colour.

To preview the printed page:

- Choose **Print Preview** from the **File** menu.

In Print Preview mode, the lower toolbar provides a variety of view options (from left to right): Zoom percent, Zoom Out, Zoom slider, Zoom In, the Zoom (region) Tool, Actual Size, and Fit Page.

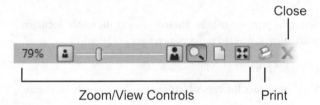

Zoom/View Controls   Print

To print:

- Click the **Print** button.

To cancel Print Preview mode:

- Click the **Close** button.

Basic printing

DrawPlus supports printing directly to a physical printer (e.g., All-in-ones, Inkjet and Laser printers) or to an electronic file such as Adobe Acrobat PDF. The printing feature allows scaling, tiling, and many other useful printing options for either method.

For the moment we'll look at basic printing to "real" printers. However, if you're working with a service bureau or commercial printer and need to provide PDF output or colour separations, see Publishing as PDF on p. 249.

To set up your printer or begin printing:

- Click ![printer icon] **Print** on the **Standard** toolbar. The Print dialog appears.

To print:

1. On the **General** tab, select a printer from the list. If necessary, click the **Properties** button to set up the printer for the correct page size, etc. Set the page size from the **Advanced** button. Depending on your printer driver, to print text with shading or custom settings, enable the "Send True Type as Bitmap" option.

2. If necessary, click the **Layout** to set options for scaling, thumbnails, multiple pages, or tiling. For details, see Printing special formats (on p. 247).

3. Select the print range to be printed—choose the whole document, current page, selected pages/page ranges as options.

4. Select the number of copies.

5. If required, save the current settings to a Print profile (see below).

6. Click **OK**.

The Preview window shows how your document maps to the selected paper size.

The pages will be printed in colour on a colour printer or in shades of grey on a black and white printer.

You can save the current combination of settings made in the Print dialog as a print profile with a unique name. Note that the profile includes settings from all tabs except the Separations tab. (By the way, don't confuse these DrawPlus "print profiles" with ICC "device profiles.").

To save current print settings as a print profile:

1. On the Print dialog's **General** tab, click the **Save As...** button next to the Print Profile list.

2. Type in a new name and click **OK**.

The settings are saved as a file with the extension .PPR.

You can restore the profile later on simply by choosing its name in the list.

Printing special formats

In Normal drawing mode, using Page Setup and printing options, you can set up pages for a variety of document types, such as Special Folded documents (greetings cards), Large documents (posters and banners), and Small documents (business cards, labels, tags). The Print dialog's **Layout** tab lets you specify other printing options, including scaling, thumbnails, multiple pages, and tiling.

Folded documents

DrawPlus automatically performs **imposition** of folded documents (cards, menus, etc.) for "Special Folded" document types. The settings ensure that two, three or four pages of the document are printed on each sheet of paper, with pages printed following the document sequence. This saves you from having to calculate how to position and collate pairs of pages on a single larger page, and lets you use automatic page numbering for the various pages.

The types most appropriate to invitations and greeting cards, include Tent Card, and Side/Top Fold Menu, Top Fold-Quarter size, Tri-Fold, or Z-Fold.

To produce double-sided sheets, check the **Balanced** option (for balanced margins) in Page Setup, then your printer's double-sided option or run sheets through twice, printing first the front and then the back of the sheet (reverse top and bottom between runs).

Printing posters and banners

Posters and banners are large-format documents where the page size extends across multiple sheets of paper. To have DrawPlus take care of the poster printing, set up your document beforehand using **File>Page Setup...** (with the "Large" document type option) to preview and select a particular preset arrangement (e.g., choose orientation).

Even if the document isn't set up as a poster or banner, you can use tiling and scaling settings (see below) to print onto multiple sheets from a standard size page. Each section or tile is printed on a single sheet of paper, and the various tiles can then be joined to form the complete page.

To print a poster or banner from a standard size page:

1. First create your standard sized page (e.g., A4).

2. On the Print dialog's **Layout** tab, check **Print tiled pages** for overlapped multiple sheets.

3. Set the **As in document** "% Scale factor" to print at a larger size (e.g. 300%).

Printing business cards and labels

While DrawPlus can deal with large-format documents it is equally suited to documents where the design can be repeated multiple times on the same page during printing. Set up your drawing beforehand using **File>Page Setup...** (with the "Small" document type option) to preview and select a particular preset arrangement.

At print time, you can set the "Multiple pages per sheet" option to **Repeat pages to fill sheet**, **Each page N times** or **Full sheet of each page** in the **Print>Layout tab**. You can tell DrawPlus to skip a certain number of regions on the first sheet of paper—useful if, for example, you've already peeled off several labels from a label sheet, and don't want to print on the peeled-off sections.

 If you haven't set up the drawing as a Small Drawing, but still want to print multiple pages per sheet, try using the **Fit Many** option.

Printing thumbnails

*   Under "Special Printing" on the Print dialog's **Layout** tab, set the "Print as thumbnails" option to print multiple pages at a reduced size on each printed sheet, taking printer margins into account. Specify the number of thumbnails per sheet in the value box.

DrawPlus will print each page of the document at a reduced size, with the specified number of small pages or "thumbnails" neatly positioned on each printed sheet.

Publishing as PDF

PDF (short for Portable Document Format) is a cross-platform WYSIWYG file format developed by Adobe to handle documents in a device- and platform-independent manner. The format has evolved into a worldwide standard for document distribution which works equally well for electronic or paper publishing.

Although PDF excels as an electronic distribution medium it is also an excellent format for delivering a drawing file to a professional printer using PDF/X formats, targeted for graphic arts and high quality reproduction. Your print partner can tell you whether to deliver PDF/X-1 or PDF/X-1a (DrawPlus supports both)—but from the DrawPlus end of things you won't see a difference. In either mode, all your drawing's colours will be output in the CMYK colour space, and fonts you've used will be embedded. A single PDF/X file will contain all the necessary information (fonts, images, graphics, and text) your print partner requires to generate either spot or process colour separations.

If professional printing is required, you'll need to select Prepress options (via the Print dialog's **Prepress** tab) before choosing to output your drawing.

To export your document as a PDF file:

1. Prepare the document following standard print publishing guidelines, taking the distribution method into account.

2. Choose **Publish as PDF...** from the **File** menu and check your export settings. (To export the whole document using default settings, you won't need to change any settings.) Make further last-minute changes (for example, a custom setting required by your print bureau).

3. Review General, Prepress, Compression, Security, and Advanced tab settings (see online Help for more details).

   When preparing a PDF/X file for professional printing, choose either "PDF X/1" or "PDF X/1a" in the General tab's **Compatibility** drop-down list, as advised by your print partner. Also inquire whether or not to **Impose pages**; this option is fine for desktop printing of a folded drawing or one that uses facing pages, but a professional printer may prefer you to leave the imposition (page sequencing) to them.

4. Click **OK** to proceed to export.

If you checked **Preview PDF file in Acrobat**, the resulting PDF file appears in the version of Acrobat Reader installed on your system.

Exporting objects and drawings

When you save a drawing, DrawPlus uses its own proprietary formats (.DPP for drawings, .DPX for templates and .DPA for animations) to store the information. From these formats it is possible to **export** your drawing as a graphic in order to read the drawing into another application or use it on a web page.

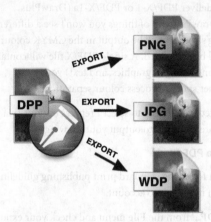

You can export at any time by using **Export as Image** or Dynamic Preview; the latter option allows editing during preview—great for pixel-accurate editing of your intended output. You can even compare side-by-side views using different export settings.

> For converting DrawPlus objects into pictures on the page, use Tools>Convert to Bitmap....

> For export as AutoCAD drawings, use Export>Export for CAD/CAM on the File menu.

Exporting as image

Especially if you're exporting web bitmap images, you can take advantage of the **Export Optimizer**, which will greatly help you in reducing file sizes and download times as far as possible while maintaining image quality. The Export Optimizer lets you export the whole page, just a selected object(s) or a user-defined region. You can also see how your image will look (and how much space it will take up) before you save it! For visual comparison, its multi-window display provides side-by-side WYSIWYG previews to compare different image formats, or the same format at differing bit depths.

To export via the Export Optimizer:

1. Choose **Export>Export as Image...** from the **File** menu.

2. (Optional) From the Export Area section, you can scale the image to a new size if desired (change **pixels**), or adjust the **dpi** (dots per inch) setting. For graphics to be used on-screen, it's best to leave these values intact. The export can be based on the whole **Page**, **Selected Area** (see Defining a region for export), or **Selected Objects**.

3. From the Properties section, select the intended graphics file format from the **Format** drop-down menu. The remaining box area will

display different options depending on your chosen graphics format. Change settings as appropriate to the file format selected (see DrawPlus help for more information).

4. (Optional) From the Web Options section, you can control web elements in your image.

    - You can uncheck Image Slices or Hotspots if you've create these elements but don't want them exported.

    - Click the **Estimate Download Time...** button to see how long the image will take to download using various connections. In the dialog, select a modem type (from 14.4 Kbps to 1.5 Mbps) in the list and the value updates immediately. You may want to keep track of the cumulative values for multiple images on a given page.

5. Click $\boxed{\text{Export}}$. If you click $\boxed{\text{Close}}$, DrawPlus remembers your preferred format and settings, particularly useful for adjusting the setting which are used if you preview the image in a browser (using **File>Preview in Browser**).

> ★ When exporting Stopframe animations, an Animation tab is shown in the dialog for frame export control.

Defining a region for export

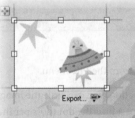

DrawPlus lets you export a specific region in your design. The region, shown as a bounding box, is actually a layer **overlay** which can be resized, repositioned over the export area and shown/hidden. The Export Optimizer is used for the actual export process.

To define an export region:

1. From the **Standard** toolbar, click [Overlays ▼] and select **Export Overlay** from the drop-down menu. A bounding box is overlaid over your page.

2. Drag a corner (or edge) handle to resize the box (use the **Ctrl** key as you drag to resize the box about its centre); reposition the box over the export area.

3. (Optional) Name the Export Overlay layer in the **Export Name** box on the context toolbar (this labels the export overlay in the Layers tab and provides the default file name at export).

4. Click [Export... ▼] shown under the box. The Export Optimizer is displayed, from which you can modify and choose an export file format (described previously).

When the overlay is applied, the bounding box is automatically selected (it shows the selection colour of the overlay layer). Clicking away from the box will deselect it (showing the box Colour), but it can be reselected at any time (e.g., for repositioning).

To select the box:

• From the **Standard** toolbar, click [Overlays ▼] and click **Export Overlay**.

Dynamic preview

Although the Export Optimizer's preview options lets you see how your export will look, it's time-consuming to repeatedly export your graphic until you get the output exactly as you want it. Instead, you can use **Dynamic Preview**, which lets you swap to a **preview-and-edit** mode, showing how your graphics will export directly on the page. It also lets you edit that output while still previewing, and set up the exported file's name, format and other settings. The ability to fine-tune object positioning to pixel level gives an added advantage for web graphics developers.

To change export settings:

1. From the **Standard** toolbar, click and choose **Preview Settings....** The option launches a dialog, which closely resembles the Export Optimizer dialog (see above).

2. Change settings on the **Format** and **Settings** tab. Settings on the Format tab change according to file type (see DrawPlus help for more information).

3. Click **OK**.

To export via Dynamic Preview:

1. From the **Standard** toolbar, click and choose **Export Preview As....**

2. From the dialog, you'll be prompted for a file name to which you can save your graphic. Choose a folder location and enter a file name.

To toggle between Normal and Preview Mode:

- Click **Dynamic Preview** from the button on the **Standard** toolbar. If you've multiple documents loaded, you'll notice the current document's tab at the top of your workspace indicate the change to preview mode, e.g.

Drawing2 *

To revert to Normal mode, click **Dynamic Preview** again.

While in this mode, any object can be manipulated or modified as if you are working in normal drawing mode, but what you're seeing is an accurate portrayal of your graphic to be exported.

Sharing via website

You can share your design by print, as a distributable electronic PDF, or via the **www.drawplus.com** website. Publishing your design to website means you can share your design and ideas with a community of like-minded designers!

The **www.drawplus.com** website is designed specifically as a design community. By uploading your completed design to the website, just like other DrawPlus users do, you add to the collection of published designs in the community.

The main website features include:

- **View published designs**

  To aid your design skills or to browse for fun, use the **Wall** design gallery which "showcases" public designs published by other DrawPlus users (...and yourself!). Take advantage of awesome **zoom** technology coupled with pan and zoom control. Easily view your own, the most recently uploaded, and most popular designs.

- **Scrapbook rating**

  Rate and comment on other people's designs—and have your own design assessed by the community. Award five stars to the very best!

- **Work in groups**

  Create groups of users with similar interests—great for schools, clubs, or maybe just your network designing friends. Use the **Group Wall** to view published designs in a chosen group, which can be private, public or "friends only." Post to **group forums** restricted to just group members.

- **Search**
  Find designs, groups, or other designers throughout the website.

- **Make new friends!**
  Social networking meets designing! Use **email** or user discussion **forums** to build friendships with other DrawPlus designers, especially those you add to your friends list. Even upload photos of yourself!

- **Profile management**
  Manage your tagline, password, timezone, language, and email notifications.

To share, three stages need to be carried out—register on the website, setup account information in DrawPlus, and then upload your chosen design to the website.

Registering for the first time

1. Click ⟨⟨ Share ⟩⟩ on the **Standard** toolbar.

2. If you've not registered before, click the **Join Now!** button. You'll be taken directly to **www.drawplus.com** registration.

3. From the website's registration form, enter your personal information, including an email address to which an activation message will be sent. Use the **Help** button if needed.

4. Click **Create Account**. For account activation, you'll need to check your email and click on the activation message sent to you. This may take time depending on your ISP and connection!

   💡 Remember your Username and Password! You'll need to re-enter this information into DrawPlus.

5. Registration is complete after activation. All that's now required is to enter your account details into your DrawPlus program (see below).

If you've already registered but not added your account details, click **Login**. This takes you to your account details where you can enter details as described in the next section.

> So you don't forget to set your user account details, you'll get a reminder to register every eight days if there are no details set. You can register on the website, then transfer your username and password over, or cancel to register later.

Setting up account details in DrawPlus

1. Select **Options...** on the **Tools** menu.

2. In the **Upload** pane, enter your remembered **Username** and **Password**.

3. (Optional) click the ⌈ **Test** ⌋ button to verify that the account details are correct. If successful, a "*Username and password valid*" message is produced.

    If you've forgotten your password or you've not already registered, use the accompanying **Reset Password** and **Register** buttons. For the latter, you'll be directed to the Registration page on the website. Complete the registration details and click **Create Account**.

4. (Optional) Reduce the upload **Quality** to 96dpi to speed up file transfer if your Internet connection is 56k dial-up modem (at the expense of zoom quality). Otherwise, use the default 300 dpi for broadband and all other faster Internet connections.

> If you change your account details on the website at a later date, you'll also need to make these account changes in DrawPlus.

Uploading

Once you've successfully created your account you can upload your design, with the option of including only specific or all pages.

☑ Page 1   ☑ Page 2

To upload your design:

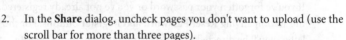

1. On the **Standard** toolbar, click 　Share　.

2. In the **Share** dialog, uncheck pages you don't want to upload (use the scroll bar for more than three pages).

3. (Optional) For the upload you can choose a different account to upload to—enter a different **Username** and **Password**. Otherwise, any previously used account will be remembered.

4. Click 　Upload　 to transfer your selected pages.

5. On upload, a progress bar indicates upload status. On completion, click **OK** to close the dialog or click **View** to immediately see your uploaded design on the website.

Index